BREAKING THE HUDDLE

Spreading the Gospel
ACROSS THE NATIONS

COURTNEY STREET

LUCIDBOOKS

Courtney's book is a clarion call to wake up the Church to the Great Task–shining the light of hope in Christ to the world. In this world of entertainment based, self-service assemblies without focus, led by CEOs rather than pastors, God still calls His people to reach the nations. I strongly recommend pastors, directors of missions, and denominational leaders read *Breaking the Huddle* and evaluate what kind of churches they have before them, making the adjustments needed to go where God is leading.

Phillip Lee Kesler
Global Mobilizing Strategist, Portland, Tennessee

There is a sinister, strategic move by the enemy of God to undermine the works of God and God's people. In this book, Courtney has shown that even some of our very Christian leaders have allowed themselves to be adversaries of God and God's Mission in the world. The good news is, this book, *Breaking the Huddle: Spreading the Gospel Across the Nations*, is a testament to this fact. This book is real and relevant; a resource tool to help the Church rise above the strategies of the enemy. I commended Courtney for this bold initiative.

Vonnie Elisha James (Reverend)
Acting Chairman Conference of Churches in Grenada W.I.

This book is dedicated to church expanders everywhere.

SPECIAL THANKS

I acknowledge and applaud the people around the world who took part in making this book possible. You all know who you are. What an honor to serve with you to get the Good News to the nations.

Let me highlight and recognize those individuals who were directly involved in getting the ideas from just a thought to the page. My wife Arleen who keeps challenging me to revisit my traditional understanding of what the Church is. She has a desire to see members of the church function as God intended. My daughter Kristen helped me formulate my thoughts as I wrestled with certain ideas. I also want to acknowledge the input of my three sons who, in their unique ways, give me glimpses into the mind of Millennials.

Thanks to Dr. Rodney Orr who supported me as he labored over the contents by reading and rereading the material. I value his suggestions and recommendations. My friend and colleague Phil Kesler put the material under the global mission microscope and helped to clarify some findings. My dear friend and brother Ralph Hardowar, a pastor in Guyana, inspired me with his dedication to God's mission for humanity. Thank you all.

FOREWORD

As I read this manuscript one thing became clear from the beginning to the end, Courtney Street loves Jesus with all his heart, and he loves the Church as well. Some things he says in this book may sound critical of the Church, but it must be understood in the context of a loving servant who is seeking to ensure that his master gets a good return on investment.

There are plenty of things the reader can get from this book that will be helpful in assessing and improving the Church's life. These must be taken in the author's contexts of love and respect for Christ's Bride. I was speaking at a men's retreat, and someone came to me and said, "You love your wife who went to be with Jesus almost a year ago more than I love mine who is still living." Why did he say this? Because his love had grown cold. He had not assessed his family situation and had let a robber come in and steal his birthright. This is what Courtney is saying about the Church. It should function just as a marriage should function because she is the Bride of Christ, and one day the marriage supper of the Lamb will take place and only Christ and his Bride, the Church, will take part in this ceremony (Revelations 19:6). Therefore, we must prepare for this great occasion by making the bride as bright and beautiful as her groom deserves. American weddings are about the bride, but this wedding supper will be about Jesus receiving all the glory.

How can we prepare for this wonderful event? By doing an occasional assessment of how the Church is progressing. Only someone who loves the Church is qualified to do this assessment, but it must be done, and Courtney has bravely stepped forward to help us do an assessment of the Church's health. Will he incur a stricter judgment for presuming to point out some of its faults? Just as the elders of churches incur a stricter judgment for presuming to teach the Word, so will those who use the Word to assess where the Church needs to grow. He isn't the first to take on this important task, but it requires each generation not only to obey God's Great Commission, but each generation must try to rejuvenate the Church in humble prayer, fasting, obedience, and worship.

Throughout history, three things are sure to follow to authenticate a movement of God among His people. First, He puts a new song in their hearts. Psalm 40:3 says, "He put a new song in my mouth, a song of praise to our God. Many will see and fear and put their trust in the Lord." New songs of worship to the Lord are sure to follow a true awakening in the Church. Second, people will put their trust in Christ. In John 17:20-21, Christ said, "I do not ask for these only, but also for those who will believe in me through their word, that they may all be one, just as you, Father, are in me, and I in you, that they also may be in us, so that the world may believe that you sent me." As new worship begins, people are drawn to trust in the Lord Jesus Christ as savior and lord. But then there must be a final authentication of a movement of the Spirit, and that is the people feel burdened with the things that burden God. The Father has given all authority in heaven and on earth to Christ, and He commands His followers to make disciples of all nations, baptizing them in the name of the Father and of the Son and of the Holy Spirit, teaching them to observe all He commanded.

Moving the Church towards fulfilling the Great Commission to make disciples is on the heart of God, and He wants it done.

This book is a call to each church to use whatever resources it must to "make disciples." The assessment urges the questions "What are we doing to build disciples?" and "What can we stop doing that does not help us in this effort?" A healthy assessment of the church may require a change to stay alive. Just like a surgeon who cuts out a cancerous growth, we must learn how to stop doing things that once helped us build disciples but no longer serve that purpose.

Race, ethnicity, denominationalism, and entertainment divide the Church and keep it from reflecting Christ's love to a lost world. They must be pulled out from the very root. Artificial growth based on numbers and not on spiritual maturity must not be seen as true growth. Satan hates this kind of renewal and will do whatever he can to keep us from it. We can't ignore the "back door" which people use to leave the Church. This back door will continue to swing widely, encouraging members to return to their old ways because there is nothing of substance to offer them.

In Jesus' 33-year ministry, he always remained focused on building his disciples. The future of the Church depended on them, as there wasn't a Plan B in case the disciples failed in their task. Just as Christ did an assessment of the seven churches of Revelations, we must also do an assessment of our local church. What areas in your church need improvement? Don't just stay in the huddle, complaining about why someone doesn't do something, but rather pick an area, talk with your church leadership, and make a difference through your service. Barna has a lot of assessment data and tools that might be helpful, and so does the Joshuaproject.net. Read this book to find out what resources are available to help your church grow. The footnotes are packed with good references for further study so be sure and read them.

Finally, I pray that reading this book will give your church a desire to love Jesus more by helping to build His Church. Nothing else in life compares to being a part of this grand design that God has placed on this earth for His glory. So, Let's "Break the Huddle" and get busy for God.

Dr. Rodney Orr

Associate Professor and Chairman of World Missions and Intercultural Studies at Dallas Theological Seminary

TABLE OF CONTENTS

INTRODUCTION

For, the earth will be filled with the knowledge of the
glory of the Lord as the waters cover the sea.

—Habakkuk 2:14

Timeouts are brief cessations of activities, intermission, or breaks, often used by parents and teachers or in sports. In sports, teams take this allotted period to gather in a huddle and stop the play clock, slow the game, substitute players, review strategy, or refocus and inspire one another to keep moving toward their collective mission . . . Winning! Teams calling timeouts to get into the huddle have proven extraordinarily beneficial and often momentum-changing, especially when their success is on the line.

As the Church[1] moves from where it is to cross the finish line, it understands its purpose and the value of timeouts. Every time it comes together, it takes a timeout to gather in a huddle. Without understanding the purpose of these recesses, God's mission for His Church is impeded.

Sports teams understand the huddle is detrimental to completing their mission. They understand the purpose of the huddle as they study the sport to become professionals. Players do not gather on the basketball court to play football or employ basketball rules. Football teams assemble on the football field and follow football rules to play the game. This is the only way they will earn the title of football champion.

Sports teams do not only understand their purpose, but they also foresee what they want to accomplish in the future. That knowledge drives their mission to win the game and become champions. Teams must break down the opponent's defenses, get into the opponent's zone, and score more points than the opponent. There is no other way to be crowned champions. They must compete in the game, follow the established rules, and complete the mission. Knowing their mission, they must answer the question, "What would it take to win?" The response will aid in the development of their game plan or strategy. Like a sports team vying for a championship, the Church understands its purpose and the rules of engagement. While the Church is not competing like sports teams, it is in competition for the souls of people. It anticipates the eternal crown of glory that will be bestowed upon it by the righteous judge (1 Corinthians 9:25). The Church knows its purpose and has a God-given vision of what He wants to use it to accomplish. God has also given it the plan to complete the mission.

The Church is God's team. The world is the "playing field" on which God calls the Church to function. The objective is to shine the light of God's glory and lead people to know the one true God and Jesus Christ whom He sent (John 17:3). The opponent is the devil, the father of lies who comes to steal, kill, and destroy (John 10:10). The objectives of the devil and his team is to hinder the Church's progress and keep people in the dark so they will not know Christ. This is where the challenge lies. The Church breaks down the enemy's defenses, but instead of scoring points, it storms the enemy's end zone and delivers the great multitude of people held in his captivity. It shines the light of God's glory in the darkness to show those in the enemy's trap the way to deliverance. But the enemy has blinded the spiritual eyes of his captives and is doing everything to prevent the Church from getting the message to them. Despite the enemy's effort, God has given the Church all it needs, including timeouts, to break down the powerful defenses of the enemy and deliver those in bondage.

Gathering regularly is a distinct characteristic of the Church. It comes together in local groups in worship as members serve and encourage one another. Members become stronger as they focus together on completing the mission. These gatherings comprise people from different nations, races, tribes, languages, and social classes. Every person in these gatherings is a gifted member of God's team—the Church. God uses these diverse individuals to advance His message to every corner of the earth. The Church takes timeouts to get into the huddle on Sundays or whenever, study, equip, and prepare members to function outside the huddle.

Since God is drawing people from diverse communities around the world, the huddle reflects diversity without discrimination. This design is to show the world that no one is exempt nor slighted by God, regardless of tribe, culture, race, or social status. With such dynamics, the huddle can never be an institution. Members are called children of God who are always on the move, intending to expand the Church from where it is to other nations. The huddle is for members to come together in worship as they empower and equip one another to serve among the nations. These members are willing to go everywhere, even into the darkest regions of the world, where they have been called to breach the enemy's gates to bring freedom to spiritual captives. Anything less would define a social club where people huddle together to meet personal needs, affirm identity, and pursue personal agendas.

The singing of praise and adoration in the assembly is only to express the worship that is already happening in people's lives.

As the Church approaches the enemy's end zone, it preaches good news to the poor and proclaims freedom for the prisoners and recovery of sight for the spiritually blind. It brings freedom to the oppressed. This is not an easy task, but the Church knows the life of followers of Christ is a perpetual reflection of Christ, so as it comes together in the huddle, members sharpen one another to shine more brightly in the world's darkness. In the huddle, it rehearses the purpose, revisits the vision, reviews its mission, reinforces strategy, and evaluates and celebrates progress. A solid game plan prepares the Church for success. It knows the value of the huddle and when to break the huddle and get back into action.

In this chaotic world, the Church's mission is more critical than ever. Human lives have become dispensable, and people in spiritual captivity have lost their desire to worship the Creator. Many are scrambling without hope and direction. In this broken world, there are few absolutes. Even political, social, or religious power has become a cheap commodity, auctioned off to those most willing to compromise truth and values. Peace and safety are popular buzzwords, but people in the enemy's captivity do not know peace. One man's disobedience brought this predicament of brokenness and chaos to the entire human race. People see God, the Creator, as the enemy and separate themselves from Him, no longer desiring fellowship with Him. In their sinfulness, they have become self-dependent and continue to search for what they cannot find. They call what is good evil, and what is evil, they call good. Without hope, they are being strangled by social, political, and religious imperialism. These systems parade people as refugees — victims in their own space. People are looking in all the wrong places, crying out for help! Nonetheless, God has given the gospel as the answer to human brokenness and entrusted His Church with bringing it to the captives.

THE PURPOSE OF THE BOOK

Jesus was taken up to heaven while His disciples stood there gazing at Him as He was taken out of sight. They stood there looking intently at the sky when suddenly, two men dressed in white appeared beside them. They asked, *"Why do you stand here looking into the sky?"* They informed the disciples, *"This same Jesus, who has been taken from you into heaven, will come back the same way you have seen Him go into heaven."* The disciples returned to Jerusalem to wait with great expectation for the authentication of their assignment and the return of their Lord.

This book is intended to encourage the local church as it pursues the assignment God has entrusted. The task has not yet been completed. Like the disciples, the local church has work to do. It cannot keep standing on the mountain top *"gazing into the sky"* waiting for the return of the Lord. This same Jesus will return, but in the meantime, churches are responsible for getting the message to every nation so that this same Jesus will return. Also, this book aims to fan the flames of revival fire and mobilize churches to reaffirm their purpose in this twenty-first-century world.

As churches enter their final countdown, they take time to get in the huddle to assess their progress. Without these periods of assessment, churches can become distracted from the mission. Taking timeouts to get in the huddle is not time to rest. Members enjoy great fellowship with one another but always prioritize completing the mission. They equip and empower one another to grow together in the knowledge and holiness of Christ so they can represent Him in the dark world. Every time they come together in the huddle, they keep casting the vision, clarifying the mission, sharpening the strategy, and rejoicing over the progress.

This book was written out of love for God's Church and crafted to help pilgrims who want to see the local church intentionally expand its proactive approach to getting the message to every individual and group. The intent of the author is to encourage, build up, empower, mobilize, and support the integrity of the local church. It is written for those who cannot be content with the status quo but want to see God's glory reflected broadly among all nations. It is to stimulate conversations about the present condition of the church in general and to help assess forward movements. As local churches engage in personal assessments, they:

- Keep casting the vision: What do they want to see God do among them?
- Keep clarifying the mission: What are they called to accomplish?
- Keep sharpening strategic actions: What will it take to complete the mission?
- Keep celebrating victories: What is the progress?

THE HOLY HUDDLE

*I myself am satisfied about you, my brothers, that
you yourselves are full of goodness, filled with all
knowledge and able to instruct one another. . . . so
that the offering of the Gentiles may be acceptable,
sanctified by the Holy Spirit.*

—Romans 15:14-16

The Church is the most significant movement since Christ
came into the world over two thousand years ago. Christ
launched the Church with the eternal purpose of gathering
the great multitude to worship before His throne. He did not
intend for the Church to be seen as a building or an institution.
The Church is people, the multitude of God's redeemed people
assembling in smaller groups all over the world. One day, this
great multitude will assemble as one Church before God's throne,
singing, *"Salvation belongs to our God who sits on the throne and
to the Lamb"* (Revelation 7:10). Until that day, the multitude of

redeemed people works together to reflect Christ from where they are to every group of people.

Christ establishes the Church's vision—a great multitude from every nation worshipping Him (Revelation 7:9). The mission is to break down the gates of hell and gather those being held hostage by sin so that they find freedom and worship God. This is pleasing to God. The strategy is simple - God gives the Church the message of the gospel to take to every group of people. This simple strategy allows the Church to become more assertive to cross the finish line. The Church empowers and deploys disciples to pull together and rescue those still bound by the enemy. As the Church leads people out of bondage, God, the owner of the Church, continues to empower the newly released and cheers them on so they can join the group of rescuers. He graciously restores His image in them and makes each renewed soul fit to worship Him.

Since its launching, the Church has continued to battle the counterattacks of the enemy. It had made significant advances at different junctures despite severe persecution and various setbacks. The innovative approaches to spiritual awakening and global evangelization continue to be noteworthy. The different drives have withstood the assaults of the enemy, who is always attempting to distract it from its game plan to force turnovers.[2] Because of its commitment to the task, multitudes of people held in bondage have been set free to enjoy new life in Christ, the *"Perfecter of faith"* (Hebrews 12:2).

In these last days of engagement, the assaults against the Church have intensified and have become more subtle. There is a serious call to the Church to stand firmly on the truth of Christ and not become distracted. The Church triumphant will remain focused. Reluctance to stand firm on the foundation of truth and remain focused will cause it to surrender its advances. The Lord, who owns the Church, designed it to keep pushing against the blockades of the enemy. It goes into the byways and snatches people from among the nations from the enemy's fire (Jude 22-23).

Taking timeouts to gather regularly in the holy huddle is a distinct characteristic of the Church. It comes together in local assemblies to worship as members serve, encourage, and have fellowship with one another. This way, members become stronger as they focus together on completing the mission. These gatherings comprise people from every nation, race, tribe, language, and social class. Every person in these gatherings is a member of God's team, the Church. They are ambassadors for Christ who have special functions. God uses these diverse individuals to advance His message to every corner of the earth. Getting into the huddle on Sundays or whenever is a means for members to be equipped and prepared for action outside the huddle.

People in the huddle have a sense of belonging and enjoy the warmth and security of the community. They learn to cultivate, nurture, love, and protect one another. Despite the security and comfort experienced in the huddle, the Church is quick to break the huddle and dive into doing the work of the ministry. It goes with the Good News to those among foreigners, asylum seekers, refugees, and all those trapped in darkness.

The enemy is intent on distracting the Church from completing the mission. In many instances, he orchestrates severe persecution to stop the Church from completing the mission. At other times, the devil entices the Church to prioritize the huddle and miss the purpose. Members are often led to believe the frequency and duration of the huddle define the quality. Some even believe they can function only when they gather in the sanctified community. They spend time fortifying temporal structures and emphasize formats over function. The message will not get to the nations when this is the case. God's people do not wait to come into the holy huddle to function as members of His Church. They come into the huddle because they are already functioning as the Church.

COMPLETE GOD'S MISSION

While the Church reviews the mission, builds up, encourages, and equips one another to complete the mission, the enemy is always trying to get the Church to abort its mission. He tried to get Jesus to do the same, but Jesus taught His Church how to complete the mission. Despite all the distractions, Jesus focused His entire life on completing His assigned mission. He could have gone into hiding with His followers and escaped the abuse He endured, but each time He got into a huddle with them, it was to help them better understand the extent of the mission. This goes beyond singing, praying, and rehearsing scriptures. He submerged Himself entirely in constant intimate conversations with the Father. He relied on the Father and did only what the Father told Him. He knew He could not complete the mission by staying in the huddle. He knew it was important to return to mingle with the often-abusive crowd. This is how multitudes would see the Father's glory.

On the "Mountain of Transfiguration" (Matthew 17), Peter, having seen Jesus talking with Moses and Elijah, thought it would be a good idea to build three tents and stay there on the mountain. This would be the safest place for them, where they could forever enjoy one another's presence. They would be away from the bothersome crowd. There, they could sing the Father's praise together unhindered. While this seemed a good idea, Jesus knew He could not complete His mission by staying secluded on the mountain, so they left and returned to the crowd.

The huddle can be a haven where members offer expressions of worship uninterrupted. There, one can enjoy protection from the harsh realities of the outside world. Jesus could have gathered

His followers and retreated to the mountains to find refuge. Or He could have stayed with John the Baptist after His baptism. After all, John had a multitude following him. It would be easy for Jesus to get lost in the large multitude following John, but He knew He would not fulfill the Father's mission by retreating to the mountains or joining John by the river. He knew the schemes of the devil but never fell to those schemes. His goal was to please the Father in everything, so He focused on the mission so that the enemy would find nothing to accuse Him of (John 14:30).

Jesus fasted for forty days and forty nights in the desert after His baptism. He was hungry and had the power to turn stones into bread. When the enemy appealed to his flesh and told Him to go ahead and turn stones into bread, Jesus rebuked him, *"Man shall not live on bread alone, but by every word that comes from the mouth of God"* (Matthew 4:4). The enemy continued to be persistent, attempting to distract Jesus. He took Jesus to the top of the temple and told him to throw Himself down since He was the Son of God. He informed Jesus the angels would protect Him, but Jesus again never fell victim to the scheme. When those approaches were unsuccessful, the Tempter then took Jesus to a high mountain and showed Him *"all the kingdoms of the world and their glory"* (Matthew 4:8). He revealed his ultimate resolve. He wanted Jesus to fall and worship him. In every case, Jesus reminded the Tempter His purpose was to worship the Father alone. He did so by listening to the Father and doing only what the Father commanded. Jesus was determined to complete the Father's mission; nothing would deter Him. Satan continues to use these same approaches he used with Jesus to tempt churches today: the lust of the flesh, the lust of the eyes, and the pride of life (1 John 2:16). As it was with the Lord, Satan continues in his attempt to tempt churches to abort God's mission by staying in the huddle.

The Church understands God's mission and undergirds its effort with trust and obedience. Only then is the holy huddle purposeful. In the garden, the first Adam was distracted from the mission and fell victim to the enemy's enticement. He aborted the mission by disobeying the Creator's command. His disobedience brought the entire human race under the condemnation of sin. Jesus, the second Adam, overcame the Tempter's enticement and stayed true to the mission. He restored trust, and now the entire human race has what it takes to obey their Creator again and be in perfect alignment with Him.

As desperate and crafty as the enemy was, he could bring no accusation against Jesus. He had "nothing" on Him (John 14:30). When the Church is engaged in doing only what the Father expects, the enemy can level no accusation against it. Jesus understood the Father's vision and passionately completed the mission. The Church must also be clear about the Father's vision and passionately seek to complete His mission and give the enemy nothing to hold against them.

In His "High Priestly" prayer (John 17), Jesus declared He had completed the Father's mission in the world. He gave people eternal life by showing them the one true God. He showed the Father to them through the work He did among them and invites the churches to show nations who He is by doing the work He gave them. The Church cannot do this in the confines of the gathering! It goes to the people, particularly those who have not yet received the message, wherever they are. It takes the message to them and gathers the multitude for God's kingdom. The ever-present Holy Spirit keeps casting God's vision to the Church as He strengthens it to complete the mission. Paul clarified the Church's mission when he reminded it as people believe in the redemptive work of Christ, they became children of faithful Abraham (Galatians 3:7). Like Abraham, his children are appointed to bless the nations as they take God's message to them.

Moses reminded the "children of Abraham" coming out of Egypt that they were God's treasured possession, a priestly kingdom, and a holy nation among all people (Exodus 19:5-6). Peter repeated this claim suggesting the Church is now God's prized possession, His chosen people, His royal priesthood, and His holy nation (1 Peter 2:9), to declare His praises among the nations. As His prized possession, He placed invaluable expectations on His Church to worship and lead others to worship Him. John described the Church (Revelation 5:10) as the kingdom of priests unto *"God and Father"* who shows God's righteous acts to all people.

Jesus commissioned His Church to give people from every nation the opportunity to hear and understand the Good News so they also might worship the Father. He empowers the Church through the Holy Spirit, who He promised would come as the Comforter (Acts 1:8). Paul restated this mission when he pointed out that God has reconciled the world to Himself through Jesus Christ and has invited His people to join Him in the ministry of reconciliation. He gave the Church the ministry of reconciliation and entrusted it with the word of reconciliation (2 Corinthians 5:18).

The Church goes to where nations are — across the street or across the world. When it chooses to break the huddle, it will never become distracted from its purpose. Taking the gospel to the nations is the only way people who have not yet heard the Good News will hear (Romans 1:16) and the only way to complete the mission.

The Church is God's final strategy for getting people among the nations to worship Him.

The harvest is ready, but there is still a shortage of true worshippers willing to go as workers in the power of Christ to complete the task. There are multitudes who take time out to gather in the holy huddle, and that is where they stay. There is joy, comfort, and security in the huddle, and many are eager to take refuge and preserve their life. The only difficulty is that, just as sports teams cannot win a game from within the huddle, the Church cannot gather the multitude from within the huddle. The Church must go to where the multitudes are. Jesus told His followers to keep praying to the Lord of the harvest to inspire churches to break the huddle and send workers to gather the multitude to worship Him. Workers go into the "harvest fields" not because it is safe or comfortable. They go because it is difficult but pleasing to the Lord. Often as workers go, they pay the ultimate price storming through the defense of the evil one, but in the end, it is all worth it. The Church runs this race with endurance, . . . *"looking to Jesus, the founder, and Perfecter of faith"* (Hebrews 12:1-2). It abandons all forms and structures that would weigh it down and returns to complete the mission as an act of worship.

SHINING WITH A PURPOSE

The wild beasts will honor me, the jackals and the ostriches, for I give water in the wilderness, rivers in the desert, to give drink to my chosen people, the people whom I formed for myself that they might declare my praise

—Isaiah 43:20-21

Some great sportspersons are described as shining in their areas of expertise. They not only make teams shine, but their aim is also to make the owners look good. Offering worship to God is the ultimate purpose of the Church. Making Christ known among the nations is its mission. After God created, He looked at His creation, and what He saw pleased Him. The heavens and the earth and everything in them reflect His beauty.

The people God created in His image after His likeness worshiped Him by showing off His supreme worth. He provided everything they needed to enhance their ability to worship. So, worship is the response of the human heart to God's holiness and is expressed not only in words but through the way people live. It is based on having the right understanding of God's nature, that He is omnipotent, omniscient, and omnipresent. Worship involves trust and obedience. Jesus talked about those who honor Him with their lips while their hearts are far from Him, making their worship vain (Matthew 15: 8-9). Worship comes from having a deep, fervent love for the sovereign Lord. It goes beyond acknowledging God for what He can do and what He has done.

When God created Adam and Eve, He desired them to trust Him. He told them they could eat from all the trees in the garden, except from the tree of knowledge of good and evil (Genesis 2:16-17). Trusting God is an act of worship. At the same time, the enemy intended to do everything to prevent the people God created from worshipping Him. Diminishing God's lordship would say He is not worthy of exclusive worship. The enemy was determined to disrupt people's worship by separating them from the Creator. He knew by separating them from their Creator, they could no longer show off God's supreme glory. He wanted them to believe they could no longer trust the Lord God.

The crafty enemy approached the woman God created and dismantled her trust in the Creator. He questioned God's instruction and challenged His conclusion. "You will not surely die. For God knows that when you eat of (the fruit) your eyes will be opened, and you will be like God, knowing good and evil" (Genesis 3:4-5). The woman then looked at the tree, and what she saw was a delight in her eyes. She desired it, believing it would make her become wise. She took the fruit, ate it, and gave some to her husband, who also ate (Genesis 3:6). Their eyes were opened, and they knew something had gone wrong. Their fellowship with the Lord was broken, and they became separated from Him.

Those who do not recognize the Creator's lordship cannot worship Him. The writer of Genesis 2 and 3 recognized the lordship of the Creator, [Yahweh Elohim – Lord God] (Gen. 2:4, 5, 7, 8, 9, 15, 16, 18, 19, 21, 22; 3:1). The Tempter, on the other hand, diminished the Creator's authority when he asked the woman, *"Did God [Elohim] actually say, 'You shall not eat of any tree in the garden?'"* (Genesis 3:1). He refused to recognize the Creator as Lord [Yahweh] and entices the woman to do same. Diminishing the Creator's authority dishonors His holiness and suggests He does not deserve to be worshipped. The Tempter led the woman to believe she could become like the Creator, to be wise, and to know good and evil. Becoming like the Creator would allow her to become her own glory, putting God's worship secondary to her personal desire.

Like Adam and Eve, all people find themselves in a state where they cannot worship the Creator. The enemy's enticement plunged people into spiritual darkness. In this darkness, hatred replaced love, and the dark shadow of sin captured people's imagination. Despite the chaos and people's predicament, the sovereign Creator, at different times and in different ways and finally, through His Church, continues to reintroduce Himself to people. Through Christ, the Creator moved to restore His image that became distorted in people so they might again fulfill their purpose. The Church is the vehicle through which those who make Jesus Christ Lord learn to worship Him. It is not unaware of the enemy's schemes and moves to strengthen its resolve to complete what it is called to do, aligning with the Creator's mission to make Himself known to nations (Revelation 3:2).

A careless Church falls victim to the enemy's enticement to reduce the lordship of Christ.

The Church continues to enjoy God's gracious blessings. Paul appealed to members of the Church in Rome to present themselves as a living sacrifice that is holy and acceptable to God. Presenting itself to God is the Church's spiritual act of worship (Romans 12:1). Everything the Church does is an expression of trust and obedience, which, is an act of worship. The Scripture admonished, "Let *us continually offer up a sacrifice of praise to God, that is, the fruit of the lips that acknowledge His name. . . . for such sacrifices are pleasing to God*" (Hebrews 13:15-16). Such sacrifices are acts of worship!

VALUE OF WORSHIPPING TOGETHER

A single member of a sports team can shine with the possession of great skills, but it is unlikely that one member of a team will win a competition. As a result, it is important the entire team gathers to play the game and make their organization look good. So, it is with the Church. It is important for individual members to live lives of worship to God, but it is also critical these members come together as one body to share in corporate worship experiences. The New Testament teaches authentic corporate worship as an extension of the worship that is already occurring in participating individuals› lives. It involves mutual relationships. As individuals share and celebrate the memorial of Christ's death and resurrection together with the anticipation of His return, they worship Him. This enhances the sense of community and gives the unbelieving world the sense of God's salvific act in a world of darkness (John 13:34). Worshipers assemble in preparation to someday stand with the great multitude of worshipers before God's throne to continue together for eternity (Revelation 7:9-10). Until then, the Church takes gets into a huddle, but does not stay there for long. It breaks the huddle to go into the world to lead many others to participate in worship. The Church disperses from its gathering to inject itself among the nations to lead people to lift their hands in adoration of the Lord as true worshipers. As the Church multiplies among nations and as people accept the saving grace of Christ, He is glorified.

THE GAME PLAN

On this rock I will build my church, and the gates of hell shall not prevail against it.

—Matthew 16:18b

C hrist wants people to know Him as their Lord and to know they can become citizens of heaven. He has affirmed their citizenship and, through the Holy Spirit, keeps drawing a great multitude to that knowledge. He appoints His Church[3] to gather this multitude from everywhere to become members and enjoy their citizen status. His game plan is to dispatch the members in smaller groups all over the world with a mandate to make Him known. These groups gather in worship in their local assemblies to strategize how they will take Christ's message to the world. As people respond to the message and are released from the enemy's captivity, they are added to the Church to expand it to the nations.

Christ redeems people by His death and resurrection and brings them into local communities called churches with the mandate to glorify Him.

As the Church multiplies and reflects the image of Christ among every tribe, language, and group, it becomes stronger. God equips members to become His ambassadors (2 Corinthians 5:20) to gather, baptize, and teach new followers to observe whatever He commands. New followers are added as the Holy Spirit resurrects conviction to equip and empower them to become ambassadors as well. Ambassadors learn to continue the process of representing Christ's interest among the nations. They inform potential citizens[4] of heaven living on earth about the offer available to them. These ambassadors are selfless and use their immunity to defend the defenseless whom the enemy is holding captive in the prison houses of the dark world. The Holy Spirit equips them to help spread the Good News of immigration to a heavenly country and about the evacuation process.

The Church should warn everyone created in God's image of eternal danger and show them how to be prepared to be evacuated before it is too late.

Since those who continue to live in the darkness often are unaware they can become citizens of heaven, Christ's ambassadors must go wherever they are to tell them of the possibility. While securing citizenship is free, it is not cheap. The Lord Jesus paid with His life. God already knows those who will accept the offer, and He is drawing them to Himself. His ambassadors gather those who will accept the citizenship offer and teach them about their spiritual citizenship. The triumphant day of worship cannot happen until Christ's ambassadors gather the last of the great called-out multitude. Local churches understand the urgency and brave whatever danger to gather every person who will stand in worship before Christ's throne.

Ambassadors sometimes behave as if they are competing among themselves and become distracted from the mission. This is pleasing to the enemy when ambassadors use fractured standards to judge and discredit one another within the community. They use doctrinal non-issues to define others and use these to decide who belongs in the body of Christ. They forget denominations and structures do not define Christ's ambassadors. Their relationship with Christ defines them. Christ Himself redeems them from the curse of disobedience to the law and by Himself pays in full for their citizenship. Christ does not judge His ambassadors by their own standards. He judges them based on His redeeming grace. Thus, all those who accept His death and resurrection and have become His followers are citizens of heaven whom He appoints His ambassadors on earth.

WHAT IS THERE TO LOSE?

In a conversation with two famous pastors, the topic of the local church expanding to the nations came up. Their response to people from their congregations who wanted to take the gospel to some unreached groups was shocking. The two pastors exclaimed they would keep members so busy in their local assemblies that they would soon forget about going to become "martyrs." How will the gospel get to people waiting to hear if God's ambassadors are reluctant to go to those who need to hear? Do these pastors understand the purpose of the Church? They justified their response by observing that lost people were coming to their doorsteps, so there was no need for members of their churches to go anywhere. They think people need to be smart. After all, according to them, "Jesus often avoided danger and escaped the crowd when they wanted to bring physical harm to Him." They implied the gospel is available and free, and people should know where to find answers to life since there are thousands of churches waiting to accommodate them. What they failed to realize if people were responding to the gospel on their own there would be no need for Christ ambassadors. Ambassadors enjoy times of furlough, in this case, in the huddle, but their assignment is carried out in the foreign field, which could be across the street. Jesus served as the greatest ambassador by leaving His home in heaven to serve in this dangerous field.

These pastors took time out every week to gather in their holy huddle and often preached about the Great Commission. They are concerned about what the enemy might do to members who go to defend those he is holding in captivity. Their concern is to guard and protect what they perceive to be their flock from physical danger. They believe they would be abdicating their positions as pastors if they allowed "their sheep" to put themselves in peril without seeking to stop them. These pastors forget those who seek to preserve their life will lose it (Luke 17:33). Jesus sent His ambassadors as lambs among wolves (Luke 10:3) because, as the Chief Ambassador, He alone can overcome the wolves and protect His lambs.

Serving Christ is not the safest thing. From the beginning, there have been many casualties among those he appointed. They gave their lives for a more lasting reward. People stoned Stephen to death for showing off Christ as Lord (Acts 7:54-60). Herod Agrippa had James executed (Acts 12:2) and imprisoned Peter. Traditions have it, they eventually crucified Peter upside down. They banished the Apostle John to the Isle of Patmos because he represented his Lord well. Today, persecution continues against those faithful enough to go into some of the darkest, most closed places with the message. Like the heroes of the faith, they looked for a "city . . . whose designer and builder is God" (Hebrews 11:10).

There are Christ ambassadors today who are driven to make Christ known despite persecution. Take, for example, the former Hindu priest who enjoyed the new life Christ gave him. He believed Christ made him new and was now a Christ ambassador. He put his life in danger to get the gospel first to his relatives, who rejected the message and persecuted him because he was willing to live out his faith in Christ. He died believing he has a place in God's kingdom. Many followers of Christ throughout the ages have given their lives to serve Christ. They were willing to lose their temporal possessions for eternal glory.

As churches equip Christ's ambassadors, they move from self-preservation to taking part in completing God's mission. Amid great danger, they see the urgency of going to the people across the street as well as across the world. They take reasonable risks, knowing they might lose what they have for the sake of expanding Christ's kingdom among the nations. The faithful martyrs looked beyond their secure walls to see the great multitude that would gather to worship.

Often, churches seek to preserve members attending the huddle while they continue to lose out in dramatic ways. By cowering behind walls of orthodoxy, they continue to lose their boldness and credibility. Many members have never experienced the joy of introducing one person to Christ. They prefer to play it safe while their neighbors near and among the nations continue to wait for deliverance from the darkness.

The message of God's love must penetrate these barriers erected to compromise, if not eradicate, the Church. The people must hear the Good News to call on the name of the Lord.

Christ wants everyone to call on His name to be saved, but how will they know to call on His name if they do not know, and how will they know if they have never heard, and how will they hear if His ambassadors are not willing to go to them? This is so important to the Lord that after He has given everything His ambassadors need, He continues to make it easier to get the message to every nation through great migration movements.

THE GREAT PEOPLE MOVEMENT

Despite persecution and severe restrictions, God continues preserving His Church and expanding opportunities to make Himself known. More than ever, people are on the move. They are moving as diplomats, students, workers, refugees, and asylum seekers. Many are migrating from countries where Christ's ambassadors have been experiencing severe persecution to places where they have the freedom to experience the gospel. This shows physical boundaries cannot restrict the movement of the Church.

There was a time when foreign missionaries were needed to go to the nations to introduce the masses to Christ. The constraints imposed on Christ ambassadors who freely share their faith stifle the spread of the gospel in many of these areas. The great people movement across the world makes it possible for many people living under religious oppression to discover life in Christ. As they experience new life, they return to their people with the Good News as representatives of Christ. This way, the gospel is spreading more rapidly to every tribe, people, group, and nation.

As churches break the huddle and arm themselves with the message, they position themselves to meet people on the move. They prepare to contextualize and communicate the message in ways the people will accept and understand. Religious high-mindedness and dogmas can often separate churches from the message, thus creating confusion in the minds of receivers. Churches do not discuss gathering the great multitude and are unwilling to make meaningful adjustments to accommodate the multitude. As true ambassadors, they meet, accept, and embrace strangers where people are —the ones socially, racially, or otherwise excluded. They do not obscure the message of their Lord by isolating themselves in their religious bubble.

The mandate of the Church must drive the message, which then gives a purpose for the gathering.

While there is the need to separate themselves from the systems of the world, ambassadors prioritize the interest of God's kingdom and do not posture themselves as isolationists. They engage the world. In His prayer (John 17:14-15), Jesus reminded His followers He gives them the mandate to function in the world although they are not of the world. He asked the Father not to take them out of the world, but to keep them in the world from the evil one. Those who promote the tyranny of Christian persecution might not like to hear the message, but Jesus does not want His Church to retreat. He entrusts the message of reconciliation to His followers to get to the nations. He broke down the walls of traditions created to insulate and isolate the Church from lurking dangers. As Jesus did, His Church meets people where they are in their brokenness and leads them to where they need to be. Jesus interacted with people in ways that, while He was never a glutton or a drunk, many associated Him with such persons. He saw value in these people. Without compromising the message, He went among them and interacted with them so they could see the Father. As the religious ones grumbled about His association with the "undesirables," He reminded them the Son of Man came to seek and to save the lost (Luke 19:9). The Church follows Jesus' example and goes among the people to gather them.

The Church has what unredeemed people need. It has the Gospel, which is God's power to salvation. Jesus invites followers to take this gospel to people everywhere and never make them feel they must come to where they gather to get what the gospel offers. People are not always aware of their spiritual neediness. Even if they do, they do not know where to go to find answers. The duty of every church is to go to the people who are languishing in separation from their Creator.

Jesus told the story (Luke 12:16-21) of how a rich man's field produced in abundance one year. The man wondered what to do with the excess. He thought to himself and concluded that he would tear down his barns and build larger ones to store all his possessions. With such great wealth, he told himself he had all the time in the world to relax, eat, drink, and enjoy his life. He had everything he needed to last him many years. The man never gave thought to sharing his possession with others. The Lord described him as a foolish man because he never thought about the brevity of life. The man died that night and could no longer enjoy his great wealth. He missed the opportunity to be purposeful among humanity, and the things he stored away could no longer benefit him.

Some followers of Christ often reflect the attitude of the rich farmer. Unreached people among the nations are calling out for help, but these churches cannot hear them. They are busy tearing down old barns to build larger and better ones. They need to think about the treasures they have been storing while not being rich toward God and His Kingdom.

In another story, Jesus talked about a man who planted a fig tree in his vineyard (Luke 13:6-8). After three years, he went looking for fruit and found none. He called one of his workers and told him to cut down the unfruitful tree. It was wasting resources. His worker appealed to save the tree for at least another year. In the meantime, he offered to dig around the tree and fertilize it to give it another opportunity to produce fruit. The worker suggested he cut down the tree if it did not produce fruit the following year.

While Christ will not cut down and cast the Church into the fire, distractions from the mission can make members become useless. A useless church is likened to an unfruitful tree. It is present, but absent in the victorious advance of the mission.

BREAKING THE HUDDLE

The man from whom the demons had gone begged that
he might be with him, but Jesus sent him away, saying,
"Return to your home, and declare how much God has
done for you." And he went away, proclaiming through-
out the whole city how much Jesus had done for him.

—Luke 8:38-39

E very time the Church gathers from life's busyness, it takes a timeout. It comes into the huddle to equip itself to complete the mission. It does not extend the timeout and take up residence in the huddle. It breaks the huddle to get the job done. Joshua Project[5] suggests there are still thousands of groups of people classified as unreached or unevangelized. Those within these groups met no one to tell them about Christ's love, and the Church has not yet met them in any meaningful way. In considering Christ's mission, the Church expands and introduces itself to these groups of people. Such expansion demands determination and dedication to the mission.

Jesus affirms whoever believes in Him will do the works He did and even greater works (John 14:12). The Church is what it is because it has been purchased by Christ. He keeps adding people who believe Jesus is Lord and that God raised Him from the dead (Romans 10:9-10). Peter describes those added as living stones who are being built into God's spiritual house to be His holy priests (1 Peter 2:5). This is important. As a kingdom of holy priests, the Church represents God to the people and the people before God. Could these greater works Jesus spoke about happen only when churches end the timeout, break the huddle, and join forces to represent God to the nations?

Players must play the game to make the timeout and the huddle worthwhile.

In different parts of the world, churches are doing the monumental works Jesus mentioned. Take, for example, one small church in an Asian country that is forced to gather late at night. At almost 3:00 a.m., the gathering dispersed one person at a time. The group huddled in the makeshift factory just after midnight for its regular meeting. Gatherers met on different days at different times of the night to reduce suspicion. Members attended as individuals appearing for work. As soon as they entered the building, they greeted one another with loving embraces and take their place in a circle of sorts on the floor. There were no chairs. Over the next few hours, the thirty-something people prayed and sang praises to the Lord in whispered tones. They studied the Scriptures[6] and discussed how they would get the message to others around them and beyond. They knew the danger of telling the Good News of Christ's salvation to their fellow countrymen, but nothing deterred them. Similar groups were being multiplied around the city and beyond within a very short time. What were they doing differently?

In their meetings, there was no music, no computer graphics, and no bright lights. A visitor could not identify the pastor since he did not occupy a place of prominence in the group. The pastor was not a paid professional and did not have an organized board of elders. These followers of Christ were risking imprisonment and even death for telling others about Jesus, yet they spent their time together, empowering and equipping one another as they worshipped. Their priority was to worship Christ by getting the Gospel to as many people as possible. This small group participated in the greater works Jesus spoke about as they multiplied themselves. They had joy and excitement and purpose despite the seriousness of being caught by the authority. They do what they need to do and then go out with greater resolve to complete God's mission. Their dedication and love for Jesus continue to lead many people to confess Jesus is Lord. Their goal is to do everything to gather the great multitude to worship. This church showed the need for the timeout to come into the huddle, which they value, but they do not linger. They find degrees of protection behind the walls of their meeting place, but they break the huddle quickly, exposing themselves to complete the mission.

On his visit to another simple church in a Middle Eastern country, a missionary became overwhelmed when He saw how loving, caring, and dedicated the members were. Despite intense persecution, the missionary encountered joy he had never experienced before. According to him, for the first time, he understood what it meant to have the joy of the Lord. The members' determination to get the Gospel to people around them and among the nations was inspiring. Like their Asian counterparts, they prepared one another to be intentional in sharing their new life story. Their goal was to multiply disciples, leading to simple churches throughout their country and beyond. They did not allow persecution or anything else to stop them. Their gathering was always purposeful, with God's vision in view. They asked the missionary about how churches were doing in other parts of the world since they were not privy to much outside news. He reported that in many countries, churches are free to gather and worship the Lord as they will. In other countries, however, churches continue to experience persecution from every side.

When the group heard there was persecution in other places, they fell to the ground in spontaneous prayer, asking the Lord to give those persecuted sisters and brothers endurance. They never prayed for deliverance from or vengeance on their persecutors. They believed persecution helped to strengthen their focus on the mission. Their government restricted their movements, but they believed their prayers could go where they could not go. They rejoiced that they were hated because they were not of the world but also because they had the privilege to show off their Lord in the world.

In the same way, there are larger congregations in places where the Church has the freedom to worship, which is also breaking the huddle. They are doing a great job in gathering the multitude to worship. Their vision is to show Christ's love across boundaries to every nation from where they are. They show their resolve to complete the mission through the time they spend in prayer for the nations, asking the Lord to open doors for the Gospel. Members have the responsibility to pray at home and in small groups for unreached groups of people, that the Lord will send workers to them to open their eyes to believe in His salvation. Like the church in Antioch (Acts 13), they regularly fasted and prayed and prepared themselves to send long-term and short-term workers from their congregations all over the world. Not only do they collaborate and network with other global mission entities, but they also dedicate a greater portion of their budget to support "global missions." Because of these involvements, over the past twenty years, more people among the nations have been calling on the name of the Lord to be saved.[7]

In every situation, the purpose of coming together should be clear. Clarity regarding the vision helps members better understand the mission, leading them to develop a sound strategic plan to accomplish the goal. In the gathering, they nurture and show their new life in Christ as they love and encourage one another. They are prepared to leave the gathering to expand the Church in the harvest fields and war zones of the world.

The strategy for winning the game involves everything players do on and off the field.

The world is a dangerous place. Being aware of the danger, Christ sends His Church into the world as lambs among wolves. Lambs are no match for ravenous wolves, yet Christ sends them anyway. The Church believes Christ the Great Shepherd has gone ahead and is protecting it as it ventures into the space of the wolves. Christ gives His Church the mandate to proclaim His Good News and provides the tools it needs in the world's turmoil. He did not send it to any place He had not gone before. He goes before and beside members of His Church as they are going to embrace the poor, mend the brokenhearted, comfort those who mourn, and open prison doors to set spiritual captives free. He is clear about the message, and the Church articulates this message to those who need to hear it.

The Church assembles itself to listen to the Lord and study His plan as He prepares it to break the huddle and go into the darkness as His light. There is joy in the huddle, but the Church does not stay in the comfort and security of the gathering. There is a greater joy in going to the world as the voice of reconciliation. Such joy is so great. Jesus informed His followers of the greater joy in heaven over one lost sinner who repents and returns to God (Luke 15:7). The Church cannot call out to the nations from behind the walls of comfort. It goes to them using every opportunity to become visible in the invisible world.

EXIT THE ECHO CHAMBERS

Some churches make coming into the huddle more important than the purpose for coming together. But the Church always remembers that Christ gives it the power to complete the mission through the Holy Spirit. Armed with this empowerment, some members take the opportunity to abuse it. They sometimes allow affluence and fame to seduce them. In their hunger for power, they appointed leaders and gathered in their fortresses to plan how to maintain their influence.

Destructive influence comes with the temptation of more pragmatic thinking, leading them to prioritize personal preferences over the Lord's mission. They decide what they think the Lord wants and not what the Lord expects. Members come together with their personal agendas, not spending much time thinking about making disciples or making Christ known. They spend the time strategizing how to always look and feel better.

The Church is on guard against the seduction of pragmatic thinking. Such thinking leads to compromise on what is affirmed as truth. In these cases, leaders focus on those in the assembly and design messages to keep people where they are - in the huddle, without concerns for the nations. Members meet with no restrictions, yet unlike those who braved danger, they come together to preach to themselves and enjoy the huddle.

Enjoying the huddle and preaching to one another is good, but to what avail? There is no room in any church for entitlement. Jesus called His people to die to self. Some, however, are turning the Church into a self-preserving echo chamber where they find comfort in talking to themselves. In this chamber, they perfected the art of comfort and entertainment. They believe the Church is a place where many people are content to sit and listen to themselves in the thriving spiritual social clubs. They are comfortable with the status quo and have little regard for those outside their circle. In the meantime, many become weary of the static routines and ask questions as they wade through the complexities of their religious experiences juxtaposed with Scriptural truths. They know there must be more to the gathering, but they do not know what it is or what to do.

Many church members are becoming tired of being spiritual spectators in the huddle and no longer see the value of being part of the local assembly. They want to be in the proverbial game, desiring relationship and purpose, so they break the huddle only to explore ways to experience and practice their faith, sometimes on their own. This is never the thing to do. In their quest, some become disillusioned and give up searching for an authentic community, the residual of the Church's failure to break the huddle. Those who are searching for the Lord with their whole heart will break the incessant huddle and find Him (Deuteronomy 4:29).[8]

THE CHURCH IS MOVING FORWARD

For I will not venture to speak of anything except what Christ has accomplished through me to bring the Gentiles to obedience—. . . but as it is written, "Those who have never been told of him will see, and those who have never heard will understand."

—Romans 15:18-21

I f the Church were a football team, people would say it possesses the ball and is moving into the enemy's end zone. The enemy is on the defensive and is attempting to take possession of the ball. He has employed all sorts of trickery to stop the Church from getting into its end zone. The Church, however, keeps on moving, doing everything to prevent a fumble. It cannot afford to turn over possession to the enemy.

A group of first-grade boys gathered around the black and neon green caterpillar. They wanted to know whether it was alive or dead. After examining the caterpillar, most of them concluded it was dead. 'It's D-dead!' ringleader Noah proclaimed.

"How do you know it's dead?" asked McGlen.

Without even looking up, Noah asked, "Is it moving? If it's not moving, that means it is dead!" They left the motionless caterpillar and went to their class.

Later that day, the boys discovered the caterpillar was moving. "It's moving! The caterpillar is moving!" joked one boy.

The first graders came running to see the miracle. As they gazed at the caterpillar in motion, Noah announced, "But it's still dead." He came to that conclusion only because he saw an army of ants carrying the caterpillar. True, the dead caterpillar was moving, but not on its own.

The Church is a living organism designed to grow and move from where it is to every nation. Christ, the architect and foundation of the Church, brings together the members as living stones in the community to build His spiritual building. He gifted these living stones with various functions and responsibilities to allow them to grow and move. Nations will know Christ as church members get to practice their spiritual giftedness. They start among themselves to build up one another and advance the Church to the nations. As members strengthen themselves from the inside, those outside waiting to call on the name of the Lord will come to know Him because a strong Church is on the move—showing off Christ.

The boys were talking about a caterpillar, but their query, "Is it moving?" can apply to local churches today. Along with resolving the question, "Is it moving?" churches must also scrutinize the types of movement. Is the movement spontaneous, arising from the prompting of the Holy Spirit, or is it a situation where it is being pushed or pulled by social and religious standards? The dead caterpillar was moving, but not because it was alive. It was being carried by the colony of ants.

Christ intended for His Church to be a movement. He did not create a religious institution to function within the confines of religious boundaries. He intended His Church to be a movement across all sectors of society. To show His intent, Jesus selected fishermen, tax collectors, and people from all walks of life to mobilize the movement. At points, the movement became so influential that the group was reported as those who "turned the world upside down" (Acts 17:5-7).

The early Church was intentional about its approach to marshaling the movement and accomplished the mandate. The movement progressed as subscribers shared the story of their new life in Christ with people they met. They worshipped the Lord in the huddle but understood the mandate to lead others among the nations to worship. These subscribers were able to do this in the context of Christ's promise to return and take them to be with Him for all eternity (John 14:1-3). They obeyed His commands, and the Church multiplied. Members could relate to the gospel's claims and benefits in personal ways when they spread what they experienced as followers.

The movement continued to spread across the region through challenging situations. The Church continued to win people of varying giftedness to support the movement. As members went along, they formed new communities, studied the apostles' teaching, and fellowshipped together. Their love for the Lord, love for one another, and even love for their enemies attracted others to accept the lordship of Christ, and they joined the movement. Those who received the message were baptized and became members of their local community of followers of Christ. The Church equipped new members, trained them, and gave them the tools needed to expand the movement to the nations.

Two thousand years later, the movement continues. God never intended His Church to become static. He continues to empower it and give it the right to be proactive. He placed it in society to set the standard for society. Local churches cannot allow the whims of secularism to govern them. The Apostle Paul instructed members not to conform to the world's systems but to keep reprograming their collective minds on God's purpose. This way, they are not distracted from representing their Master (Romans 12:2).

God gives everyone the opportunity to join the forward movement of His Church. He mandates members to use their spiritual gifts in harmony to advance the movement. Some have the task of planting or initiating, and others watering or maintaining. They work together, using their giftedness to function in fulfilling the greater purpose of expanding Christ's Church to the nations (Ephesians 4:12). Some members might be faster and stronger than others. Yet, the successful completion of the mission depends on everyone on the team.

Every movement is as strong as the weakest member of the movement.

Players in a football game perform different functions and play in various positions on the pitch. Each function must harmonize with all the others to make for a win. No one player can win the game. Every player must pool their effort together to win. Like the football team, the Church must harness the giftedness of all members to move forward effectively. It has the responsibility to train members to function in their giftedness and develop the saints to function in multiplying themselves. The message of God's redeeming love will move more rapidly to reach the corners of the earth when the Church is confident and focused on its purpose of making disciples among the nations.

Church groups meeting at Colossae, Thessalonica, and Philippi were part of the movement, and their cooperation is exemplary still today. Members were intentional about partnering together to advance the mission. Paul commended them for their faith in Christ Jesus and their love for all the saints. They had taken the Great Commission seriously, and the gospel bore fruit, and the movement increased around the world (Colossians 1:4-6). Paul saw them as imitators of Christ with the joy of the Holy Spirit. They drove God's mission through their love and commitment to Christ and to one another. These believers became examples to others even as they encountered hardship (1 Thessalonians 1:6-7). Their commitment to the mission caused multitudes to be added to the Church, and the forward movement continued.

MISSION POSSIBLE

Many people wonder whether the Church is on track to accomplish its mission. They need to look again at the early Church's history. On the day of Pentecost, Jews from different countries and regions living in Jerusalem gathered to celebrate. A small group holding to the promise of the Father to send the Comforter came together in one place. Jesus had told them to wait for the Father's promise to baptize them with the Holy Spirit to give them the power to fulfill the mission (Acts 1:4-5). When they received the power of the Holy Spirit, they became Christ's witnesses in "Jerusalem, all Judea, and Samaria, and to the ends of the earth." This appeared to be an impossible feat to make disciples of all nations. How would they complete this mission?

The disciples did not understand what to do to accomplish this impossible mission, but they trusted Jesus' words and gathered with great expectation. As promised, the Holy Spirit filled them with power, and they became bold witnesses of Christ. The small group, mainly unlearned people, speaking in all the different languages represented, spoke boldly. Hearing the message, the amazed crowd probed itself for a response. "What shall we do?" The small church gave them the answer, and three thousand persons repented and turned to Christ. That day, the movement exploded. The people who gathered to celebrate the Jewish harvest that day became part of the great harvest.

The new believers became connected to one another, and the movement continued. They took a timeout and gathered in the huddle, where they ate, studied, and prayed together. They shared their possessions with one another and splashed their love on the surrounding people. Their new life in Christ was so attractive that every day God added people to their group (Acts 2:47), and the movement grew. The same Holy Spirit is resident and active in His Church today as He seeks to multiply and expand the number of disciples in every nation.

Everyone in these communities of faith must take part in reaping and enjoying the harvest by going together from local to global fields.

Every time the Church gathers in the huddle, it reviews God's vision for the world. It rehearses and embraces God's vision, allowing itself to stay on track. It also reviews the mission and assesses the progress it is making. This review helps it remain focused as it sharpens the strategy for completing the mission. Unless believers come together to empower one another to make disciples as they are moving and disperse disciples to the nations, the enemy will slow the drive and delay the inevitable - Church getting into the enemy's end zone and destroying the strongholds.

A small church in a South American country is on the move. This church has a small congregation assembling locally, but it is on the move multiplying itself from its local community to different communities around the world. Members continue to train one another in smaller groups to make Christ known and intentionally assist them in transplanting themselves among other cultures. Some are going to different areas for employment, but their primary focus is to get the gospel to those who are waiting to hear. This small church is strategic in asking the Lord to raise up workers to go to the nations, and as He moves, they are answering the call as they go. They are completing the impossible mission. Everything they do in their assembly has global implications. They believe their success in their "Jerusalem" is a result of the concern for people to the ends of the earth. Members celebrate with joy even when their expansion meets opposition—religious, governmental, societal, or otherwise. They support those endangering their lives and taking risks to plant themselves in hostile communities. For the sake of Christ, they continue to move the Church forward, not depending on unbelievers (3 John 7). They are on the move, being driven by the Holy Spirit, unlike the dead neon caterpillar.

The dead caterpillar's movement depended on the army of ants. When anything distracts the ants, they scamper in every direction, and the work stops. The dead caterpillar is no longer able to move. So it is with a church that is not moving or is driven by temporal elements. A dead church depends on institutions, culture, traditions, and orthodoxy to carry it. God cannot use a church that is not moving. The Church of God is alive and is on the move as He uses it to fill the earth with His knowledge and influence.

MIRROR, MIRROR ON THE WALL

(Jesus) is the radiance of the glory of God and the exact imprint (image) of his nature, and he upholds the universe by the word of his power. After making purification for sins, he sat down at the right hand of the Majesty on high, having become as much superior to angels as the name he has inherited is more excellent than theirs.

—Hebrews 1:3-4

More than ever, the Church reflects the light of God's glory so that nations might see Him and rejoice. As His Church shines in obedience as it is going, the great multitude from everywhere will see Christ's glory and call on His name. His vision for people from everywhere to worship Him does not change. Everything He does is towards this end. He wants the Church to reflect His glory so people still in darkness today might see Him and come to His realm of light.

A mirror will reflect the image of an object. The image in the mirror is not the object; it is only the reflection. The reflection has no life of its own and cannot move by itself. Jesus stated that He is the light of the world and whoever follows Him will never walk in darkness but will have the light of life (John 8:12). He also informed His followers (Matthew 5:14) that they are the light of the world. Since they are in Him, they can do nothing but reflect His light in the darkness. The Church can only function through the One whose image it reflects (2 Corinthians 3:18).

GOD'S IMAGE SIGNIFIES OWNERSHIP

Christ, the head of the Church, gave His life to make it possible for the Father to restore His image in those who accept Him. Despite sin's distortion, God's image is still present in every person. Johann Christof Arnold[9] agrees, ". . . even though we have distorted this image and fallen away from God, a faint reflection remains in us." Jesus offered to restore the Father's image in every human being. As He restores His image in individuals, others will see Him and know Him. They will hear and accept the message of what Christ did to remove sin's distortion. When they believe and call on His name, He restores the splendor of His image in them.

One day, a crowd came to Jesus and inquired about the legality of paying taxes to Caesar (Matthew 22:15-22). Jesus requested a coin, and they handed Him one with the image and superscription of Caesar. Showing the coin, He asked whose image and superscription were on the coin. They told Him, "Caesar's!" Jesus then advised them to give to Caesar the things that belonged to Caesar and to give to God the things that belonged to God.

The coin bore Caesar's image, showing it belonged to him and was part of his kingdom. He had every right to do whatever he wanted with it. Caesar owned the coin, and it was his right to demand the people give it back to him. God created people in His image and likeness to show they belong to Him. He owns people and has imprinted His image on every person. He has the right to demand whatever He chooses, and He wants people to come back to Him.

Since the Church belongs to Christ, He has the authority to give the mandate to them to join Him in His work.

The Church bears the image of Christ. As it infiltrates and influences the world, it preserves the image of its owner. The world intends to do whatever it can to influence the Church to hold to the distorted image. Reflecting God's image will cost the Church, but it does not give up. It understands it is in the world on a divine mission.

How can the Church keep showing off Christ's image? It keeps on allowing the Holy Spirit to govern its mind (Romans 8:6). Knowing, desiring, and doing what Christ wants keeps the Church from being influenced by the world systems. Then the Church has the freedom to make itself a servant to all sectors without allowing itself to be led by any (1 Corinthians 9:19-23). As an example, Paul was able to infiltrate the different spheres of society and became all things to everyone, so they all had opportunities to see Christ in Him.

The descendants of Abraham took pride in defining themselves as God's chosen people. However, they failed to show off the glory of the God of their father, Abraham. They fell victim to the systems that worked against the righteousness of God, so they were not able to reflect the light of God's love to even their Samaritan relatives.

Jesus, on the other hand, understood His mission to include the rejected Samaritan people. He went into their space to show their inclusion in God's eternal plan. While the Jews avoided interaction with their Samaritan neighbors, Jesus was direct about contacting them. One day on His way to Galilee, He took the path through Samaria (John 4:4). Jesus wanted to show the Samaritan people they were just as valuable to the Father, who owned them as well.

Jesus was sitting at Jacob's well when a Samaritan woman came to get water (John 4). Jesus immediately infiltrated her space. He took the time to shine the glory of the Father in a way that enabled the woman to recognize the Father.

Jesus initiated a conversation with her, but she recognized He was a Jew. Traditionally Jews did not mix with her type, yet He asked her for a drink. To some other Jews, she was just another Samaritan woman who was an idol-worshipping half-breed. It did not matter to them that she was a person on whom God had imprinted His image. She was an outcast, so they excluded her from their space. Jesus the Messiah showed her she was no different from any other human being born in sin. He crossed the cultural, social, religious, class, and race barriers to meet her where she was and led her to see the light of God's grace. Jesus was not a Samaritan, but that day He became one, so He could more clearly reflect the Father's image to the woman. He asked her for a drink of water and showed He was willing to put His Jewish mouth to drink from her Samaritan bucket. This was unacceptable! Yet Jesus accepted her as a person. That was remarkable and a great demonstration of what the Church needs to do to reflect the Father. The light of the Father's image penetrated the boundaries of distrust and brokenness and illuminated the dark distortions in her life. Jesus used the reality of her apparent need as a bridge to bring her to the Father.

Jesus asked her to get her husband in an attempt to uncover her moral condition, and she told Him she had no husband. Some local churches would mount a condemning stance, knowing she was not truthful about her situation. Often legalism and tradition blind the eyes of churches that they cannot look beyond the distortion caused by being separated from God. Knowing her response resulted from the distorted image, Jesus responded kindly to her. He declared she was right in stating she had no husband because she indeed had five husbands, and the one she was now living with was not hers.

The woman's lifestyle did not prevent Jesus from showing her the Father's love. He was willing to eat and drink with people like her despite their stories. He approached the woman with love and not from the point of religious duty. Jesus confronted her lifestyle without condemning her. Soon she wanted to talk about her religious traditions. Jesus helped her wade through the religious maze to understand she did not have to perform rituals or go to a special place to see the Father.

So many people know about Christ without knowing Him.

The woman knew something about the Messiah, although she did not know Him. She knew He was coming and would teach them all things. Messiah was in front of her, speaking with her, yet she did not know Him. Jesus peeled away the layers of the distortion created by sin and revealed the image of the Father in her. When Jesus told her He was Messiah, the woman believed and changed her thinking about the Messiah. She immediately left where He found her and ran back to the town to tell the people, "Come, see a man who told me everything I ever did. Can this be the Christ?" (John 4:30) There was something new about her; the townspeople saw it and made their way toward Jesus. What if Jesus waited for the woman to come to Him instead of going to her? He showed His followers how they might reflect the Father as they go through life.

Sometimes church members prevent people living in darkness from seeing the Father. These church members have experienced the glory of the Father, yet they are not eager to show off His glory. They failed to bring the light of the Gospel to people wallowing in the darkness. The Church embraces the knowledge that people from every nation belong to God. Satan himself, who is the god of this world, continues to blind the minds of people as he attempts to keep them from seeing God in all His magnificence. The enemy is busy deceiving people and trying to separate them from God. The Father continues to draw people to Himself to restore His image in them, and the Church continues to gather them.

The Church uses every resource available to lead people back to their rightful owners. This is the purpose of the Great Commission. Sin distorts the Father's image and manifests itself in layers of ideologies, beliefs, and other practices. The Church understands Christ alone can remove sin's distortion. The gospel is the antidote for the poison of distortion. Christ entrusts this antidote to His Church as it embraces risks and moves into the space of people who are still waiting. Then and only then can He restore the Father's image in them.

The Gospel is God's remedy for sin's distortion.

GOD'S IMAGE REFLECTS HIS LOVE

In the first century after Christ, the church at Ephesus was a vibrant church that regularly added worshipers. Members understood their behavior became aligned with their new life in Christ. Many of them who practiced witchcraft and occult arts burned their books and artifacts in the open to show they had turned their life to follow Christ (Acts 19:19). Their actions affected the people in their community, and they spread the word of the Lord in triumph. They also discovered and showed what it meant to be a loving church. They huddled together in worship as they sought the Lord through fasting and prayer. They rehearsed their love for their Lord, for one another, and for people who needed to know Christ. In his letter, Paul reminded the Ephesians church of its inheritance in Christ and its purpose among humanity. He instructed them to function together to carry out God's mission. He confirmed their undying love for the Lord Jesus Christ (Ephesians 6:24).

Living out God's purpose for His Church is not complicated as some make it. God cast His vision and established His Church as His strategy for showing His love to the world. He empowers His Church, and His everlasting love motivates His vision and mission.

God's love transcends feelings and demands action. "For God so loved...," that He acted (John 3:16). He gave Christ as a sacrifice for people's redemption. Love costs Him everything! A popular secular song some years ago asked, "What's love got to do with it?"[10] With God and His Church, love has everything to do with it! Love reflects God's image! Love causes Him to preserve people even after they ignored Him and aligned themselves with the Tempter. God loved the world even when the world did not accept Him, and now, He shows His great love for the world through His Church. Christ's love controls His Church. He gives members the ability to spread His love to every group of people regardless of their location, race, or ideology. The world will experience Christ's love because the Church loves peoples of the world as it loves itself.

Loving one another in the community of faith is crucial to the Church because it is this love that splashes over to those who are still waiting to know Christ.

John defines the love Christ intended when he points to the sacrificial nature of such love as one "lay(ing) down his life for his friends" (John 15:13). Lest temptation drives the Church to love only those with whom it has things in common, Jesus taught members to love their enemies and to do good to those who hate them (Luke 6:27). Jesus loves every person in the world including His "enemies." He died to restore His image in them as well. The Church is ready to do the same. Members are ready to die so Christ can restore His image in lost humanity (1 John 3:16). Showing Christ's love among the nations, especially to those that are unfriendly to the Gospel, is the only way many in darkness will ever experience Him.

In the encounter with a young lawyer (Luke 10), Jesus confirmed how important it is to love the Lord God with one's entire being—heart, soul, strength, and mind. The lawyer had asked Jesus what he needed to do to inherit eternal life. Jesus challenged him, "You shall love the Lord your God with all your heart and with all your soul and with all your strength and with all your mind, and your neighbor as yourself" (Luke 10:27). Not to be outdone in the conversation, the lawyer brazenly asked, "And who is my neighbor/" (Luke 10:29). Without directly answering the question, Jesus, as was His custom, told a story about a Jewish man traveling on the road from Jerusalem to Jericho. The man was attacked by bandits, beaten up, robbed, and left half dead. A priest and then another religious leader came by. They both saw the injured man but ignored his plight. A Samaritan saw the wounded man and had compassion for him. He attended to the man, dressed his wounds, and carried him on his donkey for further treatment. To proclaim how deeply the Church loves God, it is willing to engage with its spiritually wounded neighbors.

The religious leaders who passed the injured man would surely testify of their love for God. They were involved in doing God's work in the synagogue. When the demand arose to show the Father's love to someone outside their circle, they passed it up. Their religion would not allow them to defile themselves with another's blood. They guarded their right to personal safety and preservation. The Samaritan did not seem worried about his own safety or about being castigated for attending to someone who might have been hostile to his own people. Neither history, race, nor ethnicity mattered. Humankind did. He had already purposed that he would love people, regardless of who they were, and put into practice what he had already established in his heart. When he saw the man in need, he did not care about what Jews thought of Samaritans. Love compelled him, and he was ready to assist. If loving one's neighbor resulted from loving God, which of the three in this story showed they loved God?

Jesus used this story to teach this Great Commandment involves loving neighbor as self. Loving one's neighbor as self is as important as loving God. It takes God's love to show off His image, and His love drives His mission to the nations. People everywhere will know Christ as the Church grows its love for the Father. This gives the great multitude the hope of standing before the throne to worship.

Loving others is desiring what Christ desires for them and the willingness to sacrifice for it to happen.

Jesus educated His disciples on the new commandment He gave them. They love one another just as He loved them. By loving one another, their very identity is established as His disciples (John 13:34-35).

God declares that He Himself is love. Even the Mosaic Law is about loving God and loving people. Love reaches beyond borders, real and virtual. The tyranny of politics and religion cannot stop or slow God's love from spreading to the nations. The love the Church has for God stimulates the love for people everywhere. People will get to experience God's love through His Church despite resistance. This love pierces and penetrates members' hearts with compassion and sends them to the nations despite apparent danger.

WILL THE CHURCH FUMBLE THE MESSAGE?

Some thirty years after the vibrant launch of the church in Ephesus, John revealed how that church drifted from its first love

(Revelation 2:4). The Lord Jesus commended this church for its work and patient endurance for the sake of the name of Christ. This church had a reputation for not putting up with evil and for being diligent in ministry. The leaders followed correct procedures to test those claiming to be apostles and were discerning enough to identify false ones. Yet, despite the Lord's glowing commendation, He leveled His displeasure. He said it had drifted from the love it had at first.

Could it be the once vibrant church in Ephesus became focused on internal matters and lost its passion for gathering the great multitude to worship God? Could it be they replaced their love for Christ with orthodoxy, obscuring their love for people? The Lord called this church to remember from where it had fallen, repent, and return to what drove it at first. Failing to repent had dire consequences. Any group of believers must evaluate their priorities or risk becoming obsolete to God's purposes.

The Church cloaks itself with the love of the Father and works to take His Kingdom to people everywhere. As the Church grows in love with God, it spreads this love around the world. Having compassion and showing mercy and justice to people who are different and do not share the same beliefs reflects Christ's love.

Christ's love through the Church will embrace the poor and the fatherless, accept the foreigner, and desire even the wicked to know Him.

Love for God leads people to deny themselves, give up their personal rights, and move into the space of others — even those who hate them. The Church inconveniences itself for the benefit of God's kingdom. Unless the Church presents and reflects Christ to everyone, God's perfect image will remain obscured, and Christ as King will be just an icon among traditions. People among the nations are searching for the real Christ. Most are not interested in pious stances, religious expressions, or regal structures. They want to know Jesus.

Christ gives the Church resources it needs to touch the nations in practical ways, and He is holding it accountable. He told the story (Matthew 25:31-46) about when He returns in His glory, people from all the nations will stand before Him. He will separate them into two groups. One group will be on His right and the other on the left. He will call those on his right blessed by the Father and invite them to enjoy the inheritance prepared for them. They gave away His love to strangers who were hungry, thirsty, and naked. "How is this possible?" They will ask him, *"When did we ever see you hungry and fed you, or thirsty and gave you a drink, or a stranger and welcomed you, or naked and clothed you or sick or in prison and visited you?"* The King will answer them, *"As you did to one of the least of these my brothers, you did it to me."*

THE WIDE-OPEN BACKFIELD

They went out from us, but they were not of us; for if they had been of us, they would have continued with us. But they went out that it might become plain they all are not of us.

—1 John 2:19

According to researchers, many local churches are losing members. Many of those leaving are not leaving because they have lost faith in Christ. Instead, they claimed that they lost trust in their local church. According to them, the behavior practices of fellow church members continue to erode their trust. Among those disassociating themselves from the church are those classified as Generation X, Y, and Z[11], including many of whom were brought up in the church. They leave the local fellowship as soon as they can decide for themselves.

At a regional congress, evangelical church leaders came together to find answers for what they called the "back door syndrome."[12] They were looking for answers to why the "back door of the church" seems bigger than the "front door." The leaders observed more people were leaving than were becoming members. They observed new converts were coming in the front door, but before long, many were exiting out the "back door" at an alarming rate. This backdoor syndrome describes the number of people being added to the gathering but leaving not long afterward. Many churches are doing a good job getting people in the front door, but for some reason, soon afterward, many of these same people discontinue attending the gatherings. This was a primary concern to the leaders who came together armed with several reasons for the perceived exodus. They conceded this was an age-old problem that continued to worsen with no solution. They lamented the intensity of the problem was only a sign of the times and would only get worse. The leaders, mainly older men, concluded that younger people were no longer interested in religious matters. According to them, pastors continue to preach the gospel in churches every week, but people are not coming to the church as they did in the past. They blame this phenomenon on the rise of secularism and materialism. They believe people are consumed with themselves, and their unbelieving hearts are causing some to stay away from the faith (Hebrew 3:12).

The Church does not drift from its purpose because drifting will drive it to lose its relevance in a changing society. Jesus taught His followers to make disciples as they are going and taught them to obey everything He commanded. He never instructed them to wait for people to come to them, instead He mandated them to go to the people. When disciples train new disciples to become mature disciples, they pursue the purpose of the gathering. New Believers desire to learn how to function in the reality of becoming one with Christ and one with one another. This way, they see the gathering not as a static institution but as a relevant and purposeful entity. When local churches do not invest in making believers into disciples, they will remain immature and fragile. Different opinions and "beliefisms" will distract them and cause them to depart the assembly for the simplest reasons.

Most people who abandon their local assemblies are not hostile to the Church. They are often unaware of the Church's purpose and have become preoccupied with mundane routines. They view their lives as a dichotomy and struggle to balance what they see as secular with what others purport to be religious. After years, this struggle keeps them as babies in Christ. They cannot unify the different areas of their life because they often are not grounded in the teachings of the Scripture. As a result, distractions weaken them. In these cases, church is no longer relevant to them.

Leaders continue to look for answers to the decline in church attendance. Some former churchgoers think they have the answer. They contend local church leadership is a fundamental problem. Some talked about mental abuse, while others felt alienated from leaders and decided there was no place for them in the assembly. They believe their church leaders are attempting to control them instead of equipping them for ministry. They have not experienced the freedom that comes with the gospel. Most agree leaving the church is never a suitable response, but their disillusionment has caused them to lose trust in religion. They view their exit as their only option because of the great divide between themselves and those who lead.

An informal survey conducted among people who at one time gathered with their churches shed light on a bigger problem. These former churchgoers have various explanations for leaving their churches. They use their experiences to define the "Church" as not clearly understanding the biblical definition. Although they claim the "Church is the people," they still refer to it as a building or a place. Ninety-two percent (92%) view their churches as "an institution or big business" with no interest in ordinary people or the things of the Lord. They claim pastors have been using the Church to make money, referencing some popular television pastors. These pastors present themselves as bosses and Chief Executive Officers. Others of their leaders, such as deacons and trustees, make up an executive board. According to those interviewed, they wanted to become involved in the activities of the church, but they did not have the influential power to get beyond the executive boundary. They believe they do not fit the profile of those appointed to serve.

In the results of the interview, over forty percent (40%) saw the gathering as useless or just another "social club." They accepted the Church as the people of God but believed their local church did not reflect the true Church. They further suggest their former church has little or no concern for people in the community.

Ninety-five percent (95%) of respondents between the ages of thirteen and thirty-seven assessed their church as boring and judgmental. According to them, their church sees them as young people and is not welcoming to them. They expressed feeling like an appendix and not as integrated members since there is no attempt to assimilate them into the community. In addition, they do not feel safe admitting their struggles, and they believe the church is not capable of addressing their personal issues. They felt they were unable to live up to the expectations of the older members, so they separated themselves.

Sixty-two percent (62%) of those interviewed believed their church was not spiritual enough and that something was lacking in their experiences and pressuring them into a dual lifestyle.

One person claimed he enjoyed the church while he was serving. However, that person admitted that he became tired of having to "put on his church self at church and among religious people and then having to take it off at other times."[13] He believed "church people" encourage the dual lifestyle unknowingly. He left his church because he did not feel he was "genuine, having to switch between one self to the other."

Many of these former church members believed the local church had become a political tool and was no longer "teaching the Bible." They can no longer trust a leadership that is using "God's house" to justify political agendas. When asked to give examples to support their conclusions, many claimed there are two sets of standards. While the leadership is inclined to apply the more lenient set of standards to political allies, they treat other members with indifference. This level of hypocrisy is difficult for them.

Fifteen percent (15%) of those interviewed claim they are no longer attending their church because they have become "enlightened."[14] This group of mainly young men was once active members of their churches. Now they are followers of other religions. Could this be a sign that many churches are not training members to become disciples? This is the picture given by these dissidents who were once regular attendants but now are disillusioned "backsliders" who have separated themselves from the Church.

People are looking for authenticity that will bring about a genuine change in their lives. They seek genuine fellowship where members show love and care for one another, but they often find discord and division. They want to become involved in "doing the Gospel" together in a community; instead, they become isolated spectators. According to them, their hope of getting to know the real Jesus has been dashed. Their local church never gave them that opportunity.

In the Gospels, Jesus called people to follow Him. His purpose and message were clear as He trained followers to become disciples. At one point, He told the crowd the cost of following Him, and they all retreated (John 6). He looked at the men He had been training and asked if they would also leave. They assured Him they had no place to go because He had the "word of life." Jesus taught them well. He spent about three years teaching them, and in the face of a challenge, they admitted they had no place to go but with Him. They had no desire to turn away from following Him. By the time He was ready to leave them to return to the Father, they had understood their purpose, so there was no retreating.

Jesus did life together with His disciples, but at different junctures, they encountered one challenge after another.

In their conference, the leader's reaction to the responses of these former churchgoers appeared to be shortsighted. Responders to the survey commented from their perspectives. This does not mean their observation and interpretation of different situations are correct. They were commenting from the perspective of their experience. Churches could learn from these responses since they are included in the focus. However, some leaders became defensive and critical instead of listening to them. They concluded those who expressed their desire for a perfect church would continue to be disappointed because the church is comprised of imperfect people. They missed the point. People are not looking for a church without problems. They are looking for a functional church.

Leaders at this Congress did not even start a conversation on how they could strengthen their ministry to represent Christ and meet these people where they were to lead them to where they needed to be. They preferred to continue doing what they were doing without trying to reach out to the ones wanting to become disciples. They confused the desire for authenticity and genuineness with expecting perfection. People are looking for something that is real about following Christ. As its head, Christ desires His Church to be authentic and genuine.

How will churches stop the exodus? They must create in their DNA a clear definition of the Church. From the time persons believe in Christ's resurrection and accept Him as Lord, churches should define "Church" and its function. The Church comprises individual believers who are joined together as spiritual stones in God's spiritual Body.

Having established the definition, believers in Christ need to understand the Church cannot be the Church without every believer's involvement as a living stone. These living stones gather in the huddle to develop a game plan for how best to complete the mission. Every person is important! Spiritual food and opportunities are the core of the huddle for disciples to be nourished. Exercising their spiritual giftedness and joining to advance the mission is of utmost importance. When the Church provides spiritual food, disciples will grow to maturity, discerning good from evil (Hebrew 5:14). They will stumble, but when the Church is faithful in training disciples, they will understand they belong to Christ. They will be better able to withstand storms of dissatisfaction and misunderstandings. True disciples will help one another endure challenges while developing concerns for those still waiting to know Christ. They will not leave the church to become private disciples since they know the value of the body and the urgency of the mission. They will stay and help the body harmonize its strategy and complete the mission.

Disciples who leave the church even to practice their faith privately inhibit the mission's completion. Each member has the responsibility to desire the "pure spiritual milk" of the Word (1 Peter 2:2) to grow; the Church provides the milk they need and is ready to leave the ninety-nine to pursue the one that might have strayed.

THE INTERCEPTION

"I have a few things against you: you have some there who hold the teaching of Balaam, who taught Balak to put a stumbling block before the sons of Israel, so they might eat food sacrificed to idols and practice sexual immorality."

—Revelation 2:14

That was a perfect snap! The quarterback stepped back and delivered one of the best throws of the game so far. The crowd roared with satisfaction as the ball glided through the air. Everyone thought this would end with a touchdown, for sure. Suddenly, from nowhere, a member of the opposing team sprang into the air and caught the ball. There was an interception, and the interceptor's team now took possession of the ball. An interception occurs when a player of the opposing team catches and takes possession of the ball that is intended for a player of the team who had the ball.

Like the team possessing the ball, the Church is in possession of the message of redemption. The enemy's job is to intercept the message at all costs and disrupt its forward movement to the nations. Unlike a football game where team members are easily recognized by their uniform, the enemy often disguises himself as a team member and pretends he is interested in running the message forward. He positions himself in the huddle, creating distractions to force interceptions. Here he tries to intercept the Church's vision, deconstruct its message, and change its mission. With a distorted message, he creates havoc in churches and confusion in society. However, the churches have a means of regaining the message and beginning to travel in the right direction so that others can have the chance to know Christ.

While some local churches are pursuing God's mission, others are being intercepted along the way. Christ's letters to the seven churches (Revelation 2-3) illustrate the characteristics of churches where the enemy intercepted the message. Most of the seven churches started out well, but somewhere in their experience they got distracted. Some appear impressive, yet beneath the surface are issues of inconsistencies. Despite their devotion to God, the glitter of human preferences and secular society often distract and overwhelmed them. They allow personal biases, religion, philosophy, politics, and other empty deceits to lead them away from the truth. In the effort to maintain the facade of following Christ, they add other elements to make them unrecognizable as church. They prioritize traditions and structures over truth and purpose. Many members of these hijacked churches believe they needed the things they added to attract people. In these instances, they might continue enthusiastically praising God in song, but their hearts have drifted from the truth of God's mission.

The Church is no longer passionate about what Christ cares about and often compromises the purpose.

Worship is the goal of the Church, and gathering the great multitude from every nation to worship is its mission. As an act of glorifying God in worship, the Church gets the Good News to every nation and stands firm on its purpose to fulfill this mission. It continues to move forward and pushes against the darkness, not allowing the enemy to hijack it and take possession of the message. The goal is to get the gospel beyond boundaries, cultures, and governments into dangerous and restricted communities. It must do whatever needs to be done.

While the Church continues to move forward, some allow worldly systems and aspirations to intercept the message, causing people not to worship in spirit and truth. Under the influence of their interceptor, they make compromises at the expense of God's mission.

The church at Pergamum started out well, but the system intercepted the message and purpose. This church found itself in a difficult situation. It existed where Satan ruled and was not intimidated to keep the faith. It stood firm even at the murder of Antipas, one of its faithful witnesses, and Christ commended it for its endurance. Despite its good run, some members allowed themselves to drift from the mission. They were caught up in what might have amounted to cultural Christianity, subscribing to strange doctrines (Revelation 2:14-15). As a compromising church, some members let their guard down, became complacent, and could no longer represent God's message. These members traded the truth of Christ's message for a lie as they immersed themselves in a culture that says, "Everything is good." Where did the church at Pergamum go wrong?

Churches everywhere and of all sizes can get distracted from God's mission. Often religious and social issues overwhelm them while they are giving little or no attention to their purpose. Like the church at Pergamum, churches where the message has been intercepted shift their priority from God's mission, even while having a form of godliness.

THE BIG HUDDLE

People had become accustomed to waiting in line for the second of four-morning services to adjourn. This popular suburban church attracts large groups of professionals who enjoy being at this church so much that they do not mind waiting in line in their 'Sunday best.' Who knows, the president of the United States could again be in attendance. Sometimes he would attend one of the services unannounced to the congregation. The atmosphere was that of a pop concert. Getting there early was important to guarantee the choicest seats. There was no distinction between excitement and stress anticipating the start of the service.

The time came, and those waiting were allowed into the sanctuary. The stress level increased for this first-timer who did not know what to expect. Others knew what to do and what to expect as they waited for the show to begin. The large choir facing the crowd in silence waited for the "high priest" and "council of elders" to march in adorned in their regalia. They watched the countdown clock amidst attractive computer graphics and special sound effects with excitement. Everyone waited for the performance to begin on cue. The countdown clock was counting down; five seconds, four, three, two, and on the second, the well-choreographed choir burst forth in song! The professional band and first-class production showed churches could do things with excellence.

People cheered, clapping their hands as the worship leader came to the stage. He welcomed the Holy Spirit among them in his holy tones as if the Spirit was waiting for a cue before entering. He invited the spectators to give God a handclap.

"God is in this place!" he announced. "Let us welcome Him and begin our worship! This is the place we come to worship, so leave everything outside and come let us worship." He encouraged people to raise their hands as they swayed from side to side. "Who woke you up this morning? Jesus! Who put food on your table? Jesus! Who healed you when you were sick? Jesus!" The worship leader invited the congregation to give Jesus a big hand clap and shout harder to welcome Him into their midst. The clapping was not as robust as he wanted, so he urged the congregation to cheer louder. "This time, not to me but to the Lord!" He joked.

A little later, after the choir's performance, the "shepherd of the house" (the star of the show) and his armor-bearers walked to the stage, and the congregation stood and gave thunderous applause. The Master of Ceremony further encouraged the congregation to give clap and wave offerings for the man of God. What electrifying excitement! Despite the passionate fervor, no one mentioned anything about God's mission of getting the gospel to those who are still waiting to hear. This group of congregants enjoyed the gathering but left unmindful of the multitude still waiting to hear. They came together to be encouraged and to receive their blessing but imagine what could happen if they applied the same enthusiasm to gathering the great multitude! This large congregation of worshippers could change the landscape of lostness by prioritizing God's mission. Instead, members come together in this big huddle to make their weekly oblation and claim their blessings. The pastor did a good job massaging their personal goodness and encouraged them in their worthiness. They should continue to receive the favor of the Lord and maintain their prosperity. Everything was about them. There was no expressed concern, even for their neighbor across the street who still had not yet met Christ.

THE LITTLE HUDDLE

The smaller church was not as exciting. The atmosphere was not as electrifying, but the dynamics were the same. Three ushers welcomed people into the sanctuary where they had their choice of seat. There was no line to get into the building. The entertainment production was not elaborate. There were no computer graphics, and the out-of-tune piano provided the background music. The glory days of a full house of attendees had long passed. Now, less than forty people sat in the oversized sanctuary designed to accommodate well over five hundred. The piano player directing the five-member choir begged for an "amen," while the pastor sat on the platform along with his assistant, both draped in robes, tapping their feet to the singing. The pastor waited his turn to cheer up the small crowd. At the end of the singing, the congregation applauded the choir. The crowd could see the grim expressions on the faces of the two deacons and the trustee who were seated in front of them.

Seeing what was going on stirred up a myriad of emotions. The feeling was like those experienced at the mega-church, only this time, it was not because of not knowing what to expect. The pastor came to the podium and asked the few people to give God a handclap. "God is good all the time," He announced, and the congregation responded in unison, "and all the time, God is good!"

"God is in our midst today. Let us welcome Him," the pastor went on. The congregation knew what to do because they clapped their hands to welcome the Lord. The pastor welcomed the Holy Spirit into their midst, as they did in the larger church. There was another round of applause to welcome the Holy Spirit. The pastor became the head cheerleader, trying to work up excitement among the congregation. Unlike his larger church counterpart, the pastor attempted to save the people from boredom by giving them a pep talk. He reminded the people it was God who provided for their daily needs. He informed them that God would reward those who sacrificed to support the gathering. It was another elementary feel-good message just to keep the status quo afloat. This small church was interested in many things—some good, like the winter plight of the homeless—but God's mission of getting the Good News to those waiting seemed absent from the agenda. They limited their entrusted ministry of reconciliation to their routine visitation time, and even then, the same people were visited week after week. Most of the congregation's members were baptized members of this church. Yet, the pastor attached a passionate invitation for salvation at the end of another feel-good sermon. No one responded.

Why is the decline of this local assembly of Christians so dramatic? Over ten years, this church had declined by more than 90% in attendance. At the same time, the surrounding community has seen more than 60% growth in population.

THE MORE THINGS CHANGE

This third church came a long way. A series of challenges forced it to change its approach to ministry. It was on the brink of closing its doors but made some forward-thinking changes. There was a new leader who wanted the church to reflect the racial and generational diversity of the community. He reached out with different programs like English as a Second Language (ESL) classes and after-school tutoring. Many of the former disgruntled members had returned and took an interest in the new programs. They were happy again. The contemporary band, lights, and sounds were subtle enough, not overpowering, and the atmosphere gave a coffee shop feel. The pastor, dressed in his untucked stripe shirt and sneakers, gave an inspiring message about how to avoid the stressors of the day. This was a no-nonsense huddle. Members got in, sang a few songs, prayed for one another, listened to the message, greeted one another, and were out in a reasonable time.

The entire culture of this group changed to become relevant to members. They were enjoying the new direction of their church. They were big on holy living, which was good. However, they had little interest in getting the gospel beyond the walls of their comfort. They believe it is the Church's responsibility to get the gospel to the people, but the pastor thinks they need time to heal and love one another before engaging with others. They must consider their own spiritual growth and maturity before seriously considering those who are yet to know the Lord. This had gone on for almost three years. They failed to see this stance as inconsistent with the Great Commission, where the Holy Spirit promises to make His people witnesses concentrically to the ends of the earth.

There was no line to get into the sanctuary of these smaller congregations and no countdown clock, but the gatherings of these different church models have much in common. The leaders paraded before the groups with their intrinsic timer set to get the show on the road. The job of the worship leader is to stir up the congregation, waiting to be entertained. All other laborers are relegated to the sidelines as spectators, unaware of the condition of the harvest fields. They welcomed and cheered the Holy Spirit, gave God His applause, sang enthusiastically, and called it a worship experience.

Regardless of the size of the gathering, when the church's purpose is unclear, the result is the same. The visit to these churches made one thing clear. Many attendees of churches of all sizes and orientations come together as spiritual spectators waiting to be entertained by the few. They use their feeling to assess the experience, but can anyone blame them?

ENDING THE TIMEOUT

While many churches have missed being equipped to gather those whom the Father is drawing to worship him, others are ending the timeout and are pursuing God's mission. For example, members of a large church in a medium-sized city collectively determined they would not allow anything to intercept God's purpose or His message—not even the urgency of their personal needs. Their meeting place was not but functional. Members seemed focused as they come together for their main weekly gathering. They greeted one another as they proceeded to take part in vibrant singing of praise to their Lord. Their flashy computer graphics and multi-colored lights made for a lively environment, yet not distracting. The leader led the congregation in prayer, asking the Lord to give them the endurance to be faithful. He also prayed for God to continue opening doors in their city and around the world to the gospel as well as for those who are going with the Good News. He offered a special prayer for those who had gone out from their congregation as missionaries and church planters. As he prayed, they projected pictures and silhouettes of their missionaries who had gone out from among them. This church was intentional about its mission.

Before an encouraging and challenging message from one of the elders, they were usually reminded of the large percentage of the earth's population still without a Christian witness. Asking if anyone had the opportunity to lead some to Christ, two twenty-something-year-olds popped up to the microphone to share their experiences. The elder then reminded all the members that those without the gospel were their responsibility. He gave the call to embrace their concern for their neighbors and the nations and to continue praying to the Lord of the harvest to send workers. This was their routine. Members were then separated into smaller family groups to continue their fellowship, share testimonies, and strategize with one another.

Unlike the churches that are distracted by structures and programs, this church was focused on God's mission. It built up members in righteousness and encouraged and empowered them to make disciples in their community as well as around the world. Theirs was a concurrent approach to completing the mandate. Members simultaneously became interested in the mission from their neighborhood (Jerusalem) and to the farthest nations. Their diligence and approach to finishing the Great Commission task was a realistic sign that God's Church endures enticements and does not allow the gospel message to be intercepted. They have ended the timeout and have broken the huddle and are on the field funning the message forward.

RUNNING THE MESSAGE

You are witnesses of these things. And behold, I am sending the promise of my Father upon you. But stay in the city until you are clothed with power from on high.

—Luke 24:48-49

The Church is engaged in a spiritual war, and the battlefields are the nations of unredeemed people. The enemy is fighting hard to discredit the lordship of Christ, so he keeps churches distracted. He does not entice them to engage in "big sins." Instead, he entices them to focus on establishing their own kingdoms while neglecting the mission to make Christ known to these nations. This war is not against people but against the powers of darkness and evil (Ephesians 6:12). Satan will use anything and take every measure to distract churches from their mission. The church at Thyatira is a good example of a distracted church. In His letter to this church (Revelation 2:18-28), the Lord encouraged it to be alert to the enemy's strategies. Despite its love, faith, service, patient endurance, and good works, it became distracted. This church tolerated some who subscribed to immoral practices and seductive teachings (Revelations 2: 20). When churches become focused on the mission; they are less likely to open themselves to destructive practices.

The Church does not take its mission lightly, even amidst the dangerous activities of the enemy. It does not retreat. The enemy always seeks to infiltrate a static church with seductive teachings to stop the mission, but Jesus has already given His Church what it needs to complete the mission. He demonstrates that nothing, not even death on the cross, can distract Him from completing the mission. The enemy knows of his end—eternal banishment to the pit of Hell —yet he is relentless in his attacks against the Church. He never stops! The Church, however, must anchor its focus on its Owner and keep pursuing the mission at all costs, lest it becomes complacent and indifferent.

Jesus asked the Father to keep His Church as He sends it with the message of the Good News into the world. This Good News cannot get to the people by itself. God uses His Church to broadcast the message to every nation. Before His crucifixion, Jesus talked about completing His mission in the world (John 17:3). In His high priestly prayer, He stated that He had completed His part of the Father's work and had passed on to His Church its own part. He equipped His Church and affirmed that as the Father sent Him into the world on a mission, He was sending His Church into the world on a mission (John 17:18).

Before returning to the Father, Jesus gathered with some of His followers and charged them. He reminded them the Father had given all authority in heaven and on earth to Him, indicating He was expecting them to do their part. He explained the mission to them and sent them. As He spoke to the small group of followers, they had every reason to become overwhelmed by the magnitude of the mission. Jesus understood their concern, so He promised to empower them with His Spirit, whom they would need to finish the task. They waited for empowerment, and the Holy Spirit made them His witnesses at the appointed time.

In the same way, Jesus empowers His Church today to take the Good News to people everywhere. He equips every member with various gifts to pull together in harmony to finish the task. His provision and faithfulness assure this gospel will reach the ends of the earth and that every tribe and people will hear it in their language and be represented in Heaven.

PULLING TOGETHER

Several weeks ago, the story was told of a hiker who fell off a cliff into a ravine. The rescue team's vision was to save a life. Their mission was to get the injured person out of the ravine alive. There were about fifteen rescuers, all equipped for the mission. They all took their places. Two rescuers went down the ravine while others held the ropes. Those holding the ropes shouted instructions and encouragements, asking how they were doing. After several hours of very tense communication and setbacks, they reached the injured person and did what rescuers do in these situations. Everyone was doing their part, either pulling on the rope or watching for falling rocks. Each person helped. Even the team leader stood closest to the edge of the cliff, shouting instructions and giving encouragement as they all pulled together.

Finally, they completed the rescue. Each member of the team had a special function in the team. The chief, trained to equip his team members, took part in the rescue. They all pulled together, and each did their part, leading to a successful rescue. This operation reflected how the Church goes about completing its mission. Some members will go to the nations while others hold the ropes, but completing the job calls members to do their part. God appointed the Church and each of its members to be involved in rescuing people who are in danger of eternal banishment.

Two thousand years after Christ gave the Church this major instruction, groups of people still have not yet heard the Good News to be rescued. These people are like the injured person at the bottom of the ravine, helplessly waiting for the Church to get to them! God equips the Church with the resources needed to lead the rescue. That members of the Church have not yet gone to those in the ravines of sin is an indictment. The enemy is happy to keep as many as possible from being rescued. False religions keep many mired in various spiritual bogs. Ideologies without Christ's rescue plan simply put people in bondage and give them false hope. Everyone must understand that Christ is the only one with the lifeline to rescue them. The many who are waiting to know Him and the outstretched arms of His everlasting love will feel and touch Him only through His Church.

When the Church remains steadfast in its concern for the nations, those who are perishing will hear and respond to the Good News.

God continues to invest in His Church and blesses it so it can bless the nations. He has already determined the end goal. Whether local churches are faithful to the mandate, God will complete His mission and accomplish His vision for people from every nation. He is sovereign, and His love drives Him to reconcile humanity to Himself. He continues to mold and shape His Church to complete the mission.

WHAT IS THE HOLDUP?

"Thomas, you are up!" The coach bellowed. There was some hesitation. "Thomas, what's the holdup?"

Thomas suddenly realized the coach was talking to him and took off across the field. He stopped abruptly and made an about turn to the sideline. "Coach, what am I going to do?" The crowd laughed as the second grader shouted, "Thanks, Dad!" He turned assuredly to take his position on the field.

Often, it isn't easy to complete the mission when it is unclear. Many local churches are unclear about the mission, so they become preoccupied with matters of no eternal value. God has made the mission of the Church clear. When the mission is unclear, like Thomas, the little football player, churches can consult the Coach—The Holy Spirit. The Holy Spirit will clarify the mission and provide strategic actions leading to God's good pleasure.

Everything that takes place in the assembly must lead to external engagements.

From time to time, every local church must review its structure, programs, and activities. This will help it determine how well it is fulfilling the mission. Answering the purpose question for any church ministry will help refine the focus. Some members appear to be busy, but they seldom question the purpose of their busyness. What is the purpose of activities and programs if they do not align with God's vision and mission?

Some local churches redefine the mission to reflect a political or social stance. While preserving society's health and well-being is good and might enhance the influence of these churches, this alone will not prepare people to worship before God's throne. Making life better for citizens is a noble cause, but the churches must make it the goal to go beyond and lead people to have a new life in Christ.

The Church, the spiritual descendants of Abraham, does not miss the mark like the people of Israel. God warned the Israelites continually against compromising His standards. He told them not to make a covenant with the inhabitants of the land, lest they become snares to turn them away from Him (Exodus 34:12). Traditions, cultures, and religion can ensnare churches, but they are called to maintain allegiance to God's mission. The Church does not in any way tether itself to the world's systems and agenda to be entrapped. It knows it cannot have it both ways. Christ appoints members of His Church to function as servants, working together in the Holy Spirit's power to carry out His mission in the world. Sometimes members of the Church want to insert their own individual agendas to fortify controlling positions. Yet no one can wrestle control of the Church from Christ's hands. He keeps His Church faithful as it remains true to the mission and keeps moving the message to every corner of the earth.

STAYING IN THE HUDDLE

I am sending you out like sheep among wolves. Therefore, be as shrewd as snakes and as innocent as doves. Be on your guard; you will be handed over to the local councils and be flogged in the synagogues. On my account, you will be brought before governors and kings as witnesses to them and to the Gentiles.

—Matthew 10:16-18

I magine a football team playing in the championship game. The goal of the team is to win the trophy. They envision themselves standing together after the game at the podium, holding up the trophy while the crowd cheers and the confetti falls. In their minds' eye, they visualize before the championship game even starts what they expect to experience at the end of the tournament. With this dream, they get on the field and play the game. They had learned to sharpen their strategy for completing their mission. During the game, they must get in the huddle several times to review their strategy. They call timeouts at intervals and spend short periods in the huddle.

The timeout is a timed feature of the game, so players quickly return to the field to finish the tournament. On the field, players open themselves to getting knocked down, and some suffer serious injuries. Often, injured players must be carried off the field and suspend their participation for the rest of the season, yet they always break the huddle to play the game. Players are aware of the possibility of being seriously injured in the game, yet the glory of winning the tournament takes precedence over any injury. Teams approach their mission with the end goal in mind. What might happen during the game does not intimidate them. They envision themselves at the end of the game, basking in their victory's glory.

What happens if team leaders and coaches recruit some of the best players in the league to only gather in a huddle? What if, while in the tournament, they all decided that the game was too dangerous, so they agreed to stay in the huddle for the duration of the game? Staying in the huddle would require comfortable chairs because they would need to sit for a while. Spending "quality" time in the huddle would also require food service facilities and accommodations for family members and friends. Over time, the huddle could become a permanent institution, and playing the game would no longer be the priority. They would need to maintain the huddle infrastructure. Next, they would need a fence to keep out others who might intrude. They would need to build a magnificent structure with walls and a roof to protect them from intruding elements. To sustain such a huddle, teams must keep recruiting and vetting new members. They would need additional resources to maintain the huddle. Soon, the protection and comfort they receive in the huddle would cause them to forget about playing the game. Ultimately, they would have a magnificent structure while playing the game is no longer their priority. Winning the championship would no longer be in their view. Now teams would need to adjust their vision and change their mission and strategic actions. With these actions, they would have to abandon their original aim.

Imagine players dressed in their team uniforms only to gather in their huddles. They would look professional and feel good about themselves. But what good would it be if they did not go on the field to play the game? They would be known for something, but certainly not champions of the sport. The focus and priority given to the structure of their huddle would have usurped their original purpose. The satisfaction of ownership and achievement of this new unintended structure could encourage the people to stay in the huddle and never leave.

The public would dismiss any sports team finding itself in this absurd state. They would look and sound like a team, but no one would see them as contenders because they changed their purpose to stay in the huddle and not play the game. Similarly, people would not see churches as serious partners in the gospel if they are not making and equipping disciples.

God's Church has a well-defined vision, and no one can change the mission. Christ commanded His Church to make and teach disciples as they are going among the nations (Matthew 28:19). Some members of local churches do not see the need to make disciples in obedience to Christ's mandate. Their vision is no longer the great multitude gathering to worship before the throne. In many instances, members have little responsibility in their spiritual huddle and would rather employ specialists to serve. They continue to fortify their structures to make them more comfortable. They reinforce their security and keep modernizing their programs. In words, they proclaim Jesus is Lord and that His return is imminent, but they continue to work hard to preserve the huddle as they attempt to rehabilitate society. The goal is to accumulate wealth and power while they continue to contemplate ways to repair the world's broken systems. The vision now appears to be a multitude of converts committed to gathering at regular intervals in one place to offer self-defined accolades to the Master. This new vision must now have a new strategy to evangelize those who come into their services with no outward view. Those who are accepted into their spiritual huddle will take part in preserving the empire.

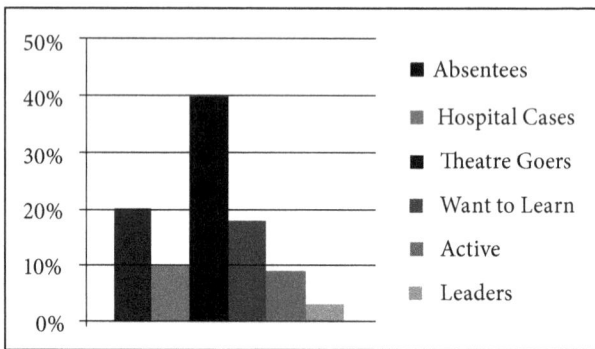

Spectators =88%; Entertainers 12%

THE CHURCH

In another informal survey of members of a popular church, twelve percent (12%) of the membership is active and functioning in their giftedness. Twenty percent (20%) are absentees. They still claim to be members but attend only on special occasions. Ten percent (10%) present themselves as hospital cases. They attend when they can but with too many health infirmities to function. They have all kinds of physical, emotional, and spiritual needs. This group includes the elderly and shut-ins. The survey further shows forty percent (40%) of the members attend the church to be "entertained." These are the theatergoers who attend only when certain persons preach or lead the worship. Six percent (6%) of those surveyed suggest they are serious about following Christ and want to learn but feel they are not qualified to serve according to the church's by-laws. Some feel they do not know enough of the Bible and are just "not yet ready." The protocol is to show up at the gathering, make sure they "pay" their tithes, and "receive a blessing." The remaining twelve percent (12%) comprises the group of active members, including leaders. Eighty-eight (88%) are fans and spectators who gather to be entertained.

This all-too-common scenario gives credence to the popular twenty/eighty rule. Twenty percent of church members carry eighty percent of the work of many local churches. This practice cannot be healthy for any church. The informal survey postulates only twelve percent of the membership of the average church is engaged. For the most part pastors, deacons, and other ministry leaders make up this twelve percent. Their function becomes more challenging as they seek to advance the ministry. In this spiritual huddle, the twelve percent is isolated from the eighty-eight percent as they are forced to carry the load. In the meantime, many see their job as guarding the eighty-eight percent so they do not drift away from the huddle. Even new converts tend to become comfortable, as religious guard rails are set up to keep them from the world, never to care for those they left behind.

The twenty/eighty rule, or in this case, the twelve/eighty-eight rule, should not apply to the Church since the Church is a living entity where every member plays an important role in carrying out the function of the body. Imagine only twelve or even twenty percent of a body's organs functioning. That person would be ill and near death. All body organs must do their part for the body to be seen as healthy. The same is true of churches. When only twelve percent of the members are functioning, churches are unhealthy and cannot fulfill their mission.

The Church does not maintain the status quo just to preserve the huddle.

The Church encourages every member to work together to build a healthy body and continues to create situations to help members understand their individual roles in the body. Members of God's Church are convinced they are like living stones being built up into God's spiritual building, where Christ is both the "Master Builder" and Chief Cornerstone (Ephesians 2:20). The Church does not set its focus on programs and activities to keep members captivated and entice others of their kind to join. The message in the huddle is clear, and members know they are all on the team. The involvement of every member determines the successful completion of the mission. As members understand Christ has ransomed them, they make it their goal to please Him. Their focus is on the heavenly city God prepared for them, and the aim is to diligently expand the Church to the nations. This is pleasing to the righteous Judge who has ready rewarding crowns.

Many members of local churches are breaking from the security of their spiritual gathering to join the Lord and His workers in the field, reconciling humanity from everywhere. They are not interested in preserving the huddle, but instead, their global passion is to find those in spiritual captivity so they can deliver the Good News to them. Their eyes are fixed on the end goal. They live daily with the expectation of seeing masses of people from neighborhoods across the street to communities far away rejoicing in the heavenly kingdom.

God does not adjust His standards to fit the ambition of misguided churches, no matter how noble their ambitions are. The coming together of believers is needful, but it is not an end. When the Church comes together in the huddle, it comes together to serve, build up and equip one another as they review God's vision. It breaks the huddle to pursue God's mission in the world.

EXPAND THROUGH SMALL GROUPS

And they went through the region of Phrygia and Galatia, having been forbidden by the Holy Spirit to speak the word in Asia. And a vision appeared to Paul in the night: a man of Macedonia was standing there, urging him and saying, "Come over to Macedonia and help us."

—Acts 16:6-9

Guy's garden was beautiful. His plants bloomed, and the flamboyant red roses painted the perfect picture of spring. He was proud of the work he had put into his garden to get it the way it was. He spent time caring for and nurturing the plants every day before and after work. He showed off his work to his horticulturist friend, who immediately noticed clusters of plants that looked good but were not doing well. The horticulturist commented on the plants in the cluster and suggested the plants were becoming unhealthy because there were too many shoots in the cluster. He recommended that Guy should transplant the shoots to keep the plants healthy. By the next spring, the transplanted plants started reproducing beautiful, healthy plants.

How similar is this to Jesus' approach to making disciples? Knowing He could spread the Good News more broadly, Jesus multiplied Himself through the selected group of twelve disciples. He poured His life into them, and as they grew in grace and knowledge of their leader, they more easily multiplied themselves among the nations. Though imperfect in their small group, these disciples learned to become proficient in advancing the mission. Jesus taught them and allowed them to practice as He equipped them for the work of the ministry. They submitted themselves to His teachings and were accountable to Him and one another. Great multitudes followed Jesus, but He focused on this small group He was preparing to expand His Church. City officials later described them as the ones who "turned the world upside down" (Acts 17:6).

In today's mega-church era, the religious community would not consider Jesus a successful church planter. This community would criticize Him regarding the size of His gathering over the period of three years. Some would give excuses for the size of His Church - only twelve men. He labored and had multitudes following Him everywhere, but He did not gather them to form a mega-church. In fact, He discouraged some from following Him. He could have proven to be a savvier church planter or church growth practitioner if He had invited the over five thousand people he fed to come to His group (John 6:1-13). Feeding the multitude could have become a strategy for instant church growth. He could start a feeding program to attract crowds of people every day. These activities would be good for those following Him but would not satisfy the purpose of His mission. Jesus intended to have His followers participate in discipling the nations, so He trained them. This smaller group of followers could rapidly multiply and be nimbler and better equipped to communicate the mission.

HOW BIG CAN YOU GO?

Jesus could set himself up as a mega-church pastor with all the perks during His time on earth. Instead, He went with His small group among the people, and He taught the masses. He trained His group of disciples, always pointing them to the Father. They would later multiply among those who need to know the Father.

When the multitude (John 6:22) returned to where Jesus fed them, He was not there. They went searching for Him across the region. This might have been a sign of genuine interest because they inquired where He had been when they found Him on the other side of the sea. Jesus knew their intentions and clarified what it meant to follow Him. They were following Him because of what they perceived He could do for them and not because they wanted to be His disciples. Jesus clarified to them that following Him required self-denial, sacrifice, and hardship. When they heard the expectations, all the people retreated. They were no longer interested in going with Him. However, his small group of twelve stayed with Him despite the pending difficulties. They had captured God's vision and believed it was their responsibility to become "fishers of men." Jesus probed their consciences, "*Do you want to go away as well?*" He asked them (John 6:67). They admitted they had nowhere else to go since they had given themselves first and fully to following Him.

How about the multitude who came to the mountainside to hear Jesus (Matthew 5)? The Bible did not tell the size of the crowd when Jesus taught the Beatitudes. What an opportunity it was to start a mega-church in Galilee! He had enough people following Him to launch such a church and accommodate the thousands of attendees. People would be glad to give their tithes to a building fund for a state-of-the-art facility. Multitudes could hear the Word and come to receive healing and deliverance. Jesus could become their leader and insulate them from the harshness of society. Instead, Jesus and His small group went to the people.

The size of Jesus› local church was only twelve men plus Himself, and they were always on the move. He trained and equipped His members in every aspect of making disciples and expanding the church while teaching and forming them spiritually. His vision always went beyond the comfort and stability of their group to embrace the entire world. He did life with this small group because He had a greater purpose than simply preserving their local community. Jesus prepared his followers to make disciples in their own community, the next town, the region, and all the way around the world. He was not interested in increasing the number of converts gathering weekly in their local synagogue. The small group size and what might have seemed to be slow growth were not indicative of a static community. His was a dynamic community where they rehearsed and practiced the mission. At the end of three years, they were trained and ready to expand to every nation.

Jesus was intentional in all He did. On the day of Pentecost, the group, grown to about one hundred twenty persons, came together in an upper room with a clear mandate. They obediently waited for the fulfillment of Jesus' promise. He had told them they would be empowered by the Holy Spirit to expand the Church to every corner of the earth. The huddle was important, but they understood they could not make disciples without going. They were serious about obeying Jesus' command and embraced God's vision of a great multitude of disciples worshipping before the throne.

The apostles understood forms and structures are temporal and were not enough to sustain the global mission thrust of the

Church. Jesus passed this knowledge to them, and they would practice what they learned. He taught them anyone who would follow Him must deny self. They understood the challenges assigned to the global purpose as their Master instructed them to go as helpless lambs among wolves (Matthew 10:16). They took nothing for their journey so as not to be impeded or become distracted from the mission. Their responsiveness to these instructions was crucial for their success.

Jesus' experiences and teachings demonstrated that church growth is measured not by the size of the local assembly but by how far the Church has expanded. The Church multiplies itself into smaller groups and spreads out as far as possible. The day will come when it gathers in one place, worshiping the King of Kings as one global Church. Then, it will remain in the huddle with the Lord forever because it has completed the task.

After the Day of Pentecost, the new church in Jerusalem, building on the foundation laid, grew as the Lord added thousands of persons being saved. On one occasion, as the Church engaged in teaching the people about Christ's resurrection from the dead, over five thousand persons believed and were added (Acts 4:4). The Church continued to expand as multitudes of both Jews and Greeks believed after hearing the Good News of Christ (Acts 5:14). This steady progression suggested the Church was doing what it needed to do to fulfill the mission.

The church in Jerusalem grew, and the Lord added members every day. The community enjoyed the benefits of the vibrant church. Christ had informed His followers they would be His witnesses in Jerusalem, but He did not stop there. He told them they would also be witnesses in all Judea, Samaria, and among all the nations of the earth. The Church does not gather in just one locale. Despite Jesus' command, the Jerusalem church became comfortable, while people in Judea, Samaria, and other nations were still waiting to hear the Good News. Christ mandated them to go beyond what was familiar to them in Jerusalem, but they were slow to go beyond. Persecution came, and that thrust the believers from the familiarity of Jerusalem to regions beyond Judea and Samaria.

Philip was among those dispersed to the city of Samaria. There he proclaimed the Good News, and the Lord added many people to the Church (Acts 8:4-8). Good things were happening in his ministry in Samaria, and there was great joy in the city (v. 8). In the middle of a revival, the Holy Spirit called Philip to another assignment, to go to the road leading to Gaza. He used Philip as a missionary to expand His Church. Few people traveled the road to Gaza, so Philip could not expect to find a crowd along this road. He chose obedience over logic and went as the Holy Spirit instructed him. He encountered an Ethiopian official reading an Old Testament text that he did not understand. Philip explained the meaning of the text and introduced him to Christ. The official believed and asked Philip to baptize him, and the Church began its expansion to Ethiopia.

In a further expansion of the Church, Paul the apostle became a part of the church at Antioch. While there, the Holy Spirit (Acts 13) prompted the church to release him and one Barnabas as their missionaries to the nations. The church fasted and prayed, and members laid their hands on the two and sent them off. Under the power of the Holy Spirit, they were instrumental in bringing people together to start new churches in different communities. After three missionary journeys, the Good News about the Messiah spread from Jerusalem all the way to Illyricum (Romans 15:19). Paul aimed to evangelize where Christ was not known, and he intentionally pushed the boundaries. Soon he stated, "... *since I no longer have any room for work in these regions, ...*" (Romans 15:23). Despite his claim, he planned to continue to expand the

Church to Spain. The church at Antioch did not all go with them on the mission, but the entire church was involved in expanding the Church to the nations. The church took ownership of the mission, and Paul and Barnabas returned to give their report.

God always placed members in the Church where some will plant, others will water, but everyone in the community will participate in celebrating the harvest. Some will go across the street while some to the nations, but the entire Church will pray, give, and send.

ARE YOU HEARING NOW?

And he said, "Then I beg you, father, to send him to my father's house — for I have five brothers—so that he may warn them, lest they also come into this place of torment."

—Luke 16:27-28

The rich man had great possessions and lived a good life. He had no reason to notice the poor man covered with sores often left at his doorstep. The poor man had no friends except the dogs, who soothed the pain by licking his sores. He yearned for the leftovers thrown from the rich man's kitchen. This poor man was in plain sight but invisible.

One day, the poor man died and was ushered into Paradise. The rich man also died and found himself tormented in hell. He looked up, and in the distance, he saw the poor man living in comfort with Abraham (Luke 16:23). In his torment, the rich man called out to Abraham to send the poor man to him to dip his finger in water and cool his tongue, but it was too late. Abraham told the rich man that the roles were reversed not long ago. The poor man had little and lived in agony, competing for food thrown from the rich man's kitchen, and he was invisible to him. He, on the other hand, lived in luxury and comfort. Now, Abraham was consoling the poor man while the rich man was left in torment. The poor man might have wanted to help quench the rich man's thirst, but a gulf between them sealed their destiny, preventing him from going to him.

The rich man then requested Abraham to send the poor man back to warn his five brothers that they might not end up in the place of torment where he was (vs. 27). There is no sign of the relationship the rich man had with his brothers while he was alive with them, but now in his death and torment, he was making the desperate appeal on their behalf. He wanted them to avoid what he was experiencing.

Could it be that the voices of countless people are crying out from the torment, beckoning the Church to take the message to the countless others who are still waiting to hear?

The poor man could not return to the rich man's brothers, but this story shows that God's people can urgently take the gospel to those who might be oblivious to their impending torment. A gulf separates heaven from hell; individuals determine where they find themselves by the choices they make. Often people make choices in ignorance, so the Church takes the responsibility to inform them so they can make the right choice. The poor man's choice to follow righteousness, despite his situation in life, secured a place for him in Paradise. He found comfort in death, and now he could not go back to the rich man's relatives. Today the world is pushed by temporal barriers such as governments, geography, religion, ethnicity, and social and political divides. It has no time to pause and hear the Church's message. Unlike the poor man, the Church continues to respond to the voice of those crying out from torment to go to those sitting in danger before it is too late. Everyone who calls to God for help gets help. But how can people call for help if they don't believe there is someone to help them? How can they know there is someone to help them if they have not heard of the One who can help them? How will they hear if no one goes to tell them (Romans 10:13-15)? God is drawing people from among the nations to Himself, and He empowers and sends His Church to tell them and gather them.

The Church is tasked with going to all those who are waiting in danger of torment, yet sometimes it is slow in going. Despite the slowness, every day God brings thousands to the steps of the local church, crying for help. They are the poor and abused, the fatherless, refugees and immigrants, drug abusers, and the homeless. They are the homosexuals and lesbians and those deceived by religion and otherworldly ideologies, thinking there is no God. They are the spiritually wounded and marginalized. They are the wealthy and affluent, all dead in trespasses and sin. They are at the mercy of churches as they wait to experience Christ's redemptive love, crying out for help. Their spiritual eyes are glazed over, and they stumble in the darkness of their brokenness, waiting to be rescued. They longed to be touched by Christ as they yearned for the crumbs of love, justice, and righteousness. Yet, all too often, churches pass them.

The Church loves and embraces broken people across the nations for whom Christ died. It does not endorse nor tolerate people's sinfulness. It sees them as Christ sees them, goes among them, and mingles with them in Christ's love as Christ did. As He mingled with broken people and went into their space the religious elites labeled Him as one of them. He did not interact with them out of pity. He accepted them and treated them with equity in their brokenness. His goal was to get them to see and accept the remedy for their brokenness. He leads broken people to understand and accept the value of being created in the perfect image of the Father who restores His image in them.

Jesus reminded the crowd that those who are sick are the ones who need a physician. He did not come to call those who are righteous to repentance. He sounds the call to those who realize they are sinners (Luke 5:31-32). Christ's Church never allows the urgency of personal comfort and security to capture and conceal its purpose to the point where sinners will not be able to experience His salvation power.

The spread of the gospel in the first century was extensive. The stalwarts of the faith were intentional in getting the gospel to the nations. Nothing stopped them! They overthrew kingdoms for the sake of the gospel. Lions, fires, and swords could not stop them. They turned disadvantage to advantage, won battles, defeated armies, and endured beatings rather than retreating. Many lost their lives in cold blood, and others became homeless, friendless, and powerless so that many nations could call on the name of the Lord to be saved. The Church keeps advancing without compromise, even under the threat of torture and death. It helps people understand only Jesus can deliver them from their brokenness and restore the image of the Father in them!

The early church was focused and intentional as it strove to bring the Kingdom of God near to the people. Members believed the words of Jesus, "... *this gospel of the kingdom must be preached throughout the entire world as a testimony to all nations, and then the end will come.*" (Matthew 24:14). They acted without fear, not counting the cost. They understood the world's possessions were temporal. As they rapidly advanced God's mission, many looked for a city that could not be destroyed instead of claiming prosperity and pseudo-security of this world (Hebrew 11:10).

Despite the world's becoming more of a global village than a great expanse of nations, multitudes still have little or no knowledge of Christ. They have not yet heard that Jesus Christ is Lord. What if churches today were as focused and intentional about spreading the Good News as their first-century counterparts? Would the great multitude have already heard? Would Christ have already returned as He promised (Matthew 24:14)? What is known is more people among the thousands of unreached groups of people would have already heard the Good News. What is preventing the rapid spread of the gospel, and why is it that over half of the world's population is still oblivious to Christ's redemptive work? Could it be churches have become comfortable in the huddle they created? These comfortable churches can neither see nor hear those in the distance who are crying out for help.

Jesus communicated the strategy, but sometimes churches have become slow to hear and too busy to care about those in spiritual distress. Churches must be active and on the move. They must listen to the cry of the lost and multiply themselves to go to them. People in torment are already crying, "Please send someone to warn those who are waiting!" Churches must go and make disciples among all nations at all costs and equip and empower disciples to move and multiply themselves!

THE FUTURE IS NOW

"Remember not the former things, nor consider the things of old. Behold, I am doing a new thing; now it springs forth, do you not perceive it? I will make a way in the wilderness and rivers in the desert. The wild beasts will honor me,..."

—Isaiah 43:18-20

Churches sometimes create their own barriers to getting the gospel to the nations. A lack of understanding of the mission and the lust for power and control often distract members from participating in the mission. This is not a new problem. The people of Israel knew they were not supposed to bow down to idols, yet as soon as they had the opportunity, they made a golden calf (Exodus 32) and committed idolatry before their God. Members today do not bow themselves to gold idols as the people did at Mount Sinai. However, they often bow to the idol of traditions, self-gratification, structures, programs, and denial. Holding tightly to these idols instead of obedience to Christ prevents them from advancing the mission.

Regardless of the condition in which these churches find themselves, God continues to preserve, rejuvenate, and empower His Church to fulfill His mission. His Church remains the workmanship of Christ, created in Him for good works, which God prepared beforehand (Ephesians 2:10). The good works reveal Christ's love for the world. The law of commandments expressed in traditions and structures can no longer govern the Church. Love for all people as God's creation and demonstrated by Christ is what drives the Church.

Jesus showed His love for sinners as He addressed the contempt of the religious leaders dragging the adulterous woman and tossing her at His feet. There was no question about her guilt. They caught her in the act of adultery, and the law demanded they stone such women. *"So, what do you say?"* They asked Jesus, ready to stone her. Jesus understood the woman's brokenness, and while not condoning her sin, He had compassion on her. He knew behind the facade of her immorality, there was the Father's image. As the leaders brought the searing accusation against her, Jesus challenged them, *"Let him who is without sin among you be the first to throw a stone at her"* (John 8:7). Blind legalism robbed them of any trace of compassion for the guilty. The law told them she deserved to die. They condemned the woman without considering their own guilt before the law and were ready to execute her. Jesus went to the extreme by showing grace and compassion. The righteous acts of the law were not enough to restore God's image in her. In fact, the righteous act would punish her. The love of the One who would give His life for her restored God's image in her. Jesus assured her He did not condemn her. His words were, "Go, and from now on sin no more" (John 8:11). This is God's heart towards sinful people. He wants them to experience His

THE FUTURE IS NOW

redemptive grace and forgiveness, which is why He lavished His grace upon members of His Church so they can extend this grace to the world.

The Church transmits grace and forgiveness and brings the kingdom of God close to sinful people.

Getting the Good News to the lost goes beyond slavish legalism to show the compassion of Christ to all people. People who are fervent about loving Christ will pursue God's mission among those who are yet to acknowledge Him as Lord. Such love guards the Church against distractions and guides it with the message of reconciliation. God's Church lets go of past experiences and presses forward with what He is doing. With the future in mind, the Church shows deep concern for reaching all groups of people with the gospel to fulfill Jesus' mission. This means churches are always rethinking their leadership structure, breaking down religious bureaucratic walls, and remaining on the watch for wolves eager to devour God's flock. This is challenging to do, but it is necessary. Churches can no longer exist in the glory days of the past. They are innovative as they make adjustments to lead people to the Savior. This takes risks and is radical in its approach.

WHO IS CALLING THE GAME?

"You know that the rulers of the Gentiles lord it over them, and their great ones exercise authority over them. It shall not be so among you. But whoever would be great among you must be your servant, and whoever would be first among you must be your slave, even as the Son of Man came not to be served but to serve and to give his life as a ransom for many."

—Matthew 20:25-28

S omeone asked at a church growth workshop, "Who is the most important person in your church?" Some said, Jesus. Others suggested the Holy Spirit. Yet some argue that pastors and elders hold the most important position because they are responsible for leading the church. Most persons concluded pastors or elders have the final say concerning the direction the church is going. They neglected to think about the fact that the Church is a body made up of many parts. Like with the human body, each part is important and has its function. If people categorized parts of the body in terms of positions, they could easily eliminate some that are not visible. Imagine what would happen to the human body if some organs were dismissed as unimportant. Likewise, God places members in the Church according to their function, so the Church gets the message of the Good News to the world. No member of the Church can be dismissed as unimportant, regardless of social or educational status.

Some people often give the impression that there are three groups in their church. There are the professional leaders, the lay leaders, and all the others. Professional leaders are usually held to a higher standard with greater accountability. They are more visible and occupy places of prominence. They are made to believe their positions make them more important than everyone else.

Lay leaders are next. They have some level of authority, and people in the church hold them to some degree of accountability. As it is with professional leaders, they sometimes guard their positions without realizing the Lord is more concerned about their functions. All other members are followers trained to be subordinate. In many churches, they seldom function in their spiritual giftedness. Whenever they do, often it is at the behest of those in charge. They feel they cannot function without the directive of the leaders. As a result, they do not participate in getting the Gospel to the nations.

Some leaders buy into this perception that they are most important and appointed to give orders because of their position in the church, while all others should do the work. One pastor informed his church that he was the shepherd, meaning he did not need to make disciples as a pastor. He continued that God called him to be the shepherd of the small congregation, while the members were entrusted with the responsibility of making sheep (disciples). According to him, the shepherd does not make sheep. "Sheep make sheep!" He further informed the church, as the shepherd, he decides in what direction the church should go since God gave him that position. Being facetious, one member asked what he would do with an unruly sheep. He explained that sometimes the shepherd must decide to "kill wayward sheep because they might cause other sheep to revolt."[15] There is every probability that it was just an illustration, but the idea of killing the wayward sheep was not clear to the congregation. Maybe he meant excommunicating the sheep, but this pervasive mentality is detrimental to advancing the mission. There is no question that the "shepherd" is tasked with giving oversight to the flock but often some are attempting to take ownership of the church.

People are asking, "Who is the leader?" When they see some who promote themselves as leaders, many choose not to follow, and they have good reasons. Jesus reminds His Church that He owns the sheep and leads them as the Good Shepherd. His sheep hear His voice; He knows them, and they follow Him. He does not slaughter His sheep. He gives them eternal life; they will never perish, and no one will snatch them from His hand (John 10:27-28). Jesus is the leader! When a sheep decides to stray, the good shepherd leaves the others to go in search of the wayward sheep. In fact, he puts himself in danger, looking for his one sheep, and invites his neighbors to celebrate with him when he finds that sheep.

Pastors are called to lead the Church in recognizing the voice of the Great Shepherd so it will not be deceived and follow strangers.

Every member of the church is important since every member, like living stones, is built into a spiritual building. Christ is both the builder and the chief cornerstone, and He connects each "living stone" so that together, they might complete the task. As the leader, He is the One who appoints and places people to function in the different areas of ministry. He appoints pastors and elders and invites them to function as shepherds. They are to exercise oversight, not dominating over those in their care, but being examples (1 Peter 5:1- 4). They recognize the voice of the Great Shepherd and teach the sheep to hear and listen to the Shepherd's voice. The flock will learn to discern the voice of the Good Shepherd and not follow strange voices.

As churches attempt to accomplish the mission, they must rethink leadership structures. Rethinking leadership structures means every member in the church setting is a leader in his or her right because of their spiritual giftedness. As members function in their areas of giftedness, they influence others to join them in actualizing the completion of the mission. However, just as God called them to lead in the areas of their giftedness, they must be followers in other areas. This renders every member a follower at one time or another.

When the need arose in the early church, the members looked to the apostles to resolve the issues. Instead of taking on the task of caring for the dissatisfied widows, the apostles summoned all the disciples to consider the issue (Acts 6). They instructed the church to select seven men gifted in service and allowed them to take care of the situation. The apostles did not make the selection. God placed in the group people gifted in areas of administration and service, and the church selected them to serve as deacons. The deacons then functioned in their giftedness while the apostles continued to give attention to prayer and the word ministry. There was no competition or subordination. There was no boss or worker. For the advancement of the body no one was more important than the other. They functioned in their areas of giftedness together. Teaching, equipping, and watching over the saints were the apostles' functions in the church. The entire group, including the deacons, came under their leadership as they taught. The deacons gave attention to the neglected widows and saw they were taken care of. As they served, the apostles placed themselves under the deacons' leadership in administration and hospitality.

The apostles recognized the deacons' authority and did not dictate to them how to perform their assigned tasks. They became followers in those instances. This did not diminish their own authority as teachers. They had the confidence that they had equipped the deacons with words to perform their duties. The apostles taught them well and did not have to intervene in administering their duties. This principle applies to all aspects of the Church's ministry.

The Church must re-think its leadership structure and break down the religious bureaucratic wall.

BREAK DOWN BUREAUCRATIC WALLS

One day the mother of James and John came kneeling before Jesus asking that He allow her two sons to sit by Him in His kingdom, one at His right hand and the other at His left (Matthew 20:21). Sitting beside Jesus in His kingdom would no doubt elevate them to positions of prominence. Jesus was direct in His response, telling her she did not know what she was asking. He reminded His disciples though they were leaders, they were first servants. Leaders among unbelievers seek to exercise control over others. Jesus taught His disciples this is not to be so in His Church. Leaders should imitate Christ, who did not come for others to serve Him but He to serve others and to give his life as a ransom for many (Matthew 20:28).

Churches cultivate environments of servants. Jesus is the great leader, yet He presented Himself as an obedient servant to the people. He broke down the bureaucratic walls so the gospel could reach people where they were. Churches sometimes try to rebuild invisible walls that Christ has already broken down.

Often these walls create a divide between those who lead and others. These walls protect the few elevated to certain positions while preventing the masses from functioning as part of a church.

Every member of the Church is a leader in some stage of development. They are developing in their areas of giftedness to carry out the mission. Leadership involves influence, and members are leaders because they allow the Holy Spirit to lead them in their sphere of giftedness. They influence others to follow them as they follow Christ and take part in making and teaching disciples. While the world might have seen Jesus' disciples as a group of ordinary fishers, Jesus saw them as leaders. He called them to follow Him. He trained them and gave them the opportunity to function, and they changed the world. Together, they built up one another to be all they could be to fulfill God's mission and equip one another to equip others as well (2 Timothy 2:2).

Pastors have been given the responsibility to equip the saints to do the work of the ministry while watching over them. (Acts 20:28, 1 Peter 5:2). Their giftedness includes nurturing, teaching, guiding, and giving members tools they need to optimize their gifts. They are not bosses, as some understand. They are interested in seeing members grow towards maturity, where they are empowered to practice their spiritual gifts freely. Jesus showed this principle when He entrusted the mission's leadership to those He equipped. He told them what to do and showed them how they should do it. He assisted them, watched them as they practiced, and then left them knowing they were equipped to do the job. Even after Jesus left them, the disciples still showed levels of immaturity in some areas, showing they were still developing.

Developing members are like student doctors. They are skilled in presenting theories but are not recognized as doctors until they practice what they have learned. The same is true for church members who are equipped to serve. Until they start to serve, they cannot be called disciples. They must practice what they learned.

While pastors give oversight to the saints' development, they might not function as leaders in other ministries of the church. For example, every church member should be hospitable, yet not everyone has the gift of hospitality. In such cases, pastors who do not have the gift of hospitality are better off coming under the leadership of those who are gifted in areas of hospitality. They recognize those whom God raised to serve and faithfully follow them for the sake of advancing God's mission.

Christ is the leader of His Church, and everyone else is a servant. To practice the act of serving, the church must reconsider the traditional structure and adjust.

The Pyramid Model

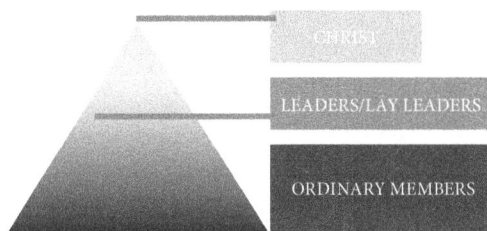

The Pyramid Model is a popular model of the structure of churches. In this model, Christ is the head and is at the peak. Denominational leaders follow, falling under Christ. Pastors and other ministry leaders follow in the hierarchy of importance. Ordinary members of the laity make up the base. In this model, leaders are treated as mediators between Christ and the laity. They often present themselves as the ones who hear from God on behalf of members and pass down His instructions. Some of these leaders define success by the number of people at the base. They train members to rely on them to discern the voice of the Holy Spirit.

They erroneously confer on themselves titles of bishop, prophet, and apostle and elevate themselves outside of proper biblical context. In these instances, members become docile and remain spiritual babies, depending on these leaders while absolving themselves from their spiritual responsibility.

The Circle Model

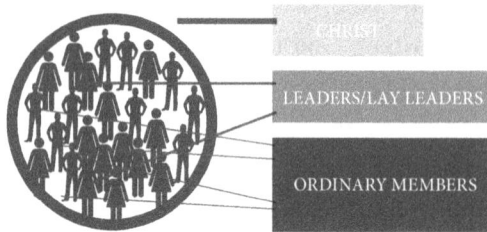

The circle model seems to be a better illustration of the structure of the Church. It illustrates inclusiveness. The outside circle represents Christ, who is still the head of the Church. His body comprises members whom the Father draws to Himself (John 6:44). Christ connects them to one another in His body (Romans 12:5). Every member is on the same level of acceptance to the Lord. No one is more important than the other. In the body, Christ gives all these ordinary members gifts to use to accomplish the body's mission. He appoints apostles, prophets, evangelists, pastors, and teachers to function as trainers to watch over and equip members to exercise themselves in righteousness, do the work of ministry, and lead in building up one another in the body of Christ.

In this model, there are no minority or majority positions. Positions are less definite as members carry out their functions. The function of each person is complementary to the others as they work together towards the same goal. Pastors take the lead in equipping and watching over the saints while all the other members join in sharpening pastors in this function. Pastors cannot do the equipping and watch by themselves. Members must encourage them as they encourage and build up one another to excel in all their functions. This leads to the willingness to submit to one another.

While the functions are not equal, everyone is equally accountable to one another and to the Lord. No one can function independently and expect the body to move. Every function supports the others for the church to move forward. With these principles in mind, it might be helpful for churches to rethink some of the existing leadership structures. Pastors, bishops, and overseers must give up their status as bosses and Chief Executive Officers and desire to become servants themselves. Jesus identified Himself as a servant, and Paul, the apostle, introduced himself as a servant. Becoming servants might not be a popular thing among some leaders, but they must give up the desire for power and leadership perks. They can no longer allow ego and prestige to stop them from becoming servants.

As servants, they will do the dirty jobs like washing the feet of others instead of demanding others wash their feet. They will not clamor for honor but seek to serve well. As leaders, they will know how to follow and not seek to take the lead in everything. They respect the giftedness of others and empower, encourage, support, and motivate members to lead according to their giftedness. They accept that others in the body are more competent in certain areas than they are. This means they will continue developing themselves to equip the saints to serve. When they empower others to function in their giftedness, they are also empowering themselves.

Christ is the only one who can lead His Church to accomplish its mission in the world. Recognizing they are mere servants, leaders of churches must hand the Church back to Christ, the great Shepherd, and recognize Him as the only Shepherd. Pastors are not the shepherd. The Good Shepherd calls them to do the work of the shepherd. This will encourage them to break down the religious bureaucratic wall that creates separation in the body. They will want to relinquish positions, titles, high places, and egos to return to a place of servanthood. As servants who embrace God's vision for people, they will still seek to protect churches from wolfish intruders who are eager to stop the gospel from getting to the nations.

While leaders are busy securing and solidifying their leadership positions, the utmost yearning of the enemy of Christ is to render the Church dysfunctional. He is famous for deploying these wolfish intruders amid the flock to render the sheep complacent or scatter them and cause them to become defenseless. Jesus warned His followers (Matthew 7:15) about the false prophets who would come among them looking like sheep but were sheep devourers. They create distractions and cause division in the body of Christ.

Paul also expressed concern for doctrinal disruption in the body and particularly addressed the "super-apostles" who were creating divisions in the Corinthian church (2 Corinthians 11:1-13). He expressed his dismay that as the serpent deceived Eve by his cunningness, he could lead believers away from pure devotion to Christ. He also expressed his concerns for the church in Galatia, as the members were quickly deserting Christ and turning to another gospel, which according to him was no gospel of Christ (Galatian 1:6). People were coming among them, trying to distort the message. He warned them not to subscribe to teachings contrary to what they had learned. Such contrary teachings would cause division and disrupt the mission of the church. In the same way, he encouraged the Ephesian elders to pay careful attention to those whom the Holy Spirit had given them (Acts 20:28). He warned them they needed to be alert because some masquerading as equippers would come in among them, speaking twisted things to draw them away.

In his second letter, Peter also wrote about false prophets and false teachers who would come to the church.[16] He pointed out they would secretly come into the huddle bringing with them destructive heresies, even denying the Lord Himself. Unfortunately, many people will follow these false leaders in their sensuality and blasphemy. Their words, ways, and promises can be enticing, but the consequence is detrimental.

How do churches guard against these ravening wolves? First, churches must learn to discern the signs. These wolves care only for themselves, seeking power and building their names and empires. They will destroy the sheep (John 10:10-13) to actualize their personal goals. They have little concern for the great multitude from everywhere, spending their energy on marketing and elevating themselves, their agenda, and achievements.

Although leaders are vested with the responsibility to lead in communicating the vision and mission of the church, every member has the responsibility to watch out for the wolves. Pastors and teachers in the assembly must train members to become competent in discerning God's will. At the same time, members have the responsibility to "long for the pure spiritual milk" (1 Peter 2:2). They must become skillful in using God's Word to guard their hearts and remain alert and be about the King's business. Every follower of Christ must be diligent in becoming scholars of the scriptures, knowing who the Lord is, who he or she is in Him, and what He expects in the relationship. They will more readily recognize the wolves as they embrace, study, and hide God's Word in their heart.

Local churches need all their parts working together in harmony to function best (Ephesians 4:15-16). That is how they grow together in Christ, who is the head. When each part of the body works, the body will grow and build itself up in love. Unity causes the body to function more purposely toward God's mission, enhancing growth and expansion. Disunity in the body disconnects the flock and stifles the church. A fragmented church is competitive on all levels and is distracted from what God has called it to do.

Completing God's mission in the world demands that churches try to connect Christ's followers with one another. Paul, writing to the church in Rome, told them, "... *so we, though many, are one body in Christ, and individually members one of another.*" (Romans 12:5). Many assemblies are intentional about creating situations to enhance unity and connecting members with one another. They bypass religious preferences and traditions and emphasize the mission, knowing every member needs to function to finish the mission.

Small groups are ideal for connecting God's flock. In these small groups, twelve to fifteen members would commit to sharing life together for about four to six months at a time. They gather to study the scriptures, fellowship, and encourage and build up one another to live in ways that are honoring to the Lord. At the end of this period, several members from each group would rotate into other groups to repeat the process. Groups are responsible for making disciples and teaching new disciples to make disciples as well. As they make disciples, they form additional groups to accommodate and integrate new members. They will repeat this process multiplying themselves.

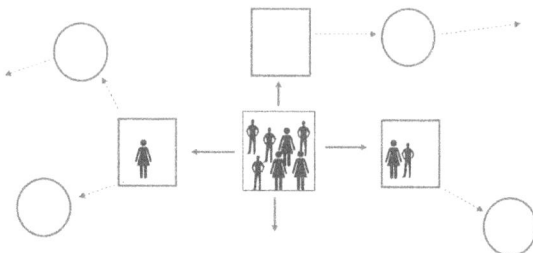

The Church expands through small groups multiplying from one community to another as they spread the gospel. While members are going as missionaries from these smaller groups, the entire church is responsible for supporting them. The goal is to multiply the Church and expand it to the nations. The Church is engaged when members leave to go to more distant places to show off Christ. This is part of connecting the local flock with one another, even to the ends of the earth.

Not only is it important to fellowship and train members, but it is also critical to include every member in clarifying the mission. Every age group in the church should have a seat at the table where they can listen to one another's input and give their own insights. It is more difficult for members to fall through the cracks and easier for them to use their gifts in building up and connecting with one another.

In many ways, the early Church showed this principle of connecting the flock. Members came together and devoted themselves to the apostles' teaching as they fellowshipped with one another. They found time to eat together, prayed together, and had everything in common as they addressed everyone's needs. They served and built up one another as they shared in the mission. Members saw themselves as a connected unit, sharing in one another's grief and joys. They did life together and met the needs of other Christ followers while they themselves were being challenged. Despite one church's poverty and struggles, members gave ungrudgingly to the needs of those far away who might at one time have even been better off than them. This is only possible when churches understand members are not defined by denominations but by being members of Christ's body. Members everywhere must embrace the one vision and understand how important it is to work together as a universal unit to complete the mission.

Churches in many places are experiencing severe persecution, but because they fall under different denominations, they are sometimes ignored by the larger body and detached from believers in other areas. Churches must familiarize themselves with these sufferings. This way, they can pray for those suffering Christians wherever they are, that they endure the test and afflictions. Churches must be marked not only by prayer and encouragement but also by empathy and love toward one another. They must endeavor to share their needs and help meet some of them.

The Church lives out its connectedness with Christ and one another for those who continue to live in the darkness to see the glory of Christ's image and understand His grace. Through the connectedness of churches, members will work together to bring the kingdom of God closer to the nations. They will partner together to gather the great multitude to worship the King. John noted this global connectedness in his third letter. He expressed his great joy hearing those believers were walking in the truth. He further commended their faithfulness in connecting with brothers and sisters, even though they were strangers. As a demonstration of their love, they sent "them on their way in a manner that honors God," so they did not need to depend on receiving help from Gentiles (3 John 1:6-7). This way, churches show hospitality on a global basis, connecting the saints to work together for the truth.

BREAK DOWN DIVIDES

I appeal to you, brothers, by the name of our Lord
Jesus Christ, that all of you agree, and that there be
no divisions among you, but that you be united in the
same mind and the same judgment.

—1 Corinthians 1:10

Most people will not die from being hit by a truck. People take precautions and get out of the way of the moving truck. It is a known fact most people will become sick and die from diseases that are invisible to the naked eye. Cancer is developed from radical cells in the body that have gone rogue. They separate themselves from normal cells and operate on their own. When this is the case, those cells create chaos in the body. Infected persons would have liked to see and deal with them before they could do any damage. This confirms the idea that "it is not always the big things that cause the greatest problem. The little things do." Often churches take precautions against big threatening things they can see while overlooking the small things that are more deadly to the body. Even though it's not a small thing, division in and among churches is one of the most insidious threats. Knowing the negative consequences of divisiveness, followers of Christ frequently become complacent and choose sides. The enemy exploits personal biases to undermine the mission's effectiveness among the nations.

Right from the beginning of time, the enemy has always used persecution as an external strategy to weaken the function of the Church. Instead of bringing the Church to its knees, persecution against the Church only strengthens it. This is nothing new. In the letters to the seven churches in Revelation, persecution could not stop the forward movement of the Church. Having found this to be an impossible strategy, the enemy employs the more subtle strategy of "divide and conquer" to drain spiritual energy and weaken the body.

Division, a silent killer, prevents churches from showing God's power in the world. The enemy uses members to maintain these divides and put one group against another. The believers in Corinth used their religious preferences as dividing lines to determine who was in and who was out. They not only expressed disagreements but also separated themselves into religious tribes to quarrel about who was for whom. After greeting them in his first letter, Paul appealed to members not to allow divisions among them. While not promoting uniformity, he encouraged them to unite in the same mind and judgment (1 Corinthians 1:10).

There are many dividing lines drawn by churches, each leading to a destructive end. Personal preferences are designed to put wedges between members to immobilize the mission. One of the most divisive threats to the mission is racial division. This division is subtle, giving people the idea some people are "more saved than others" because of their race. The time has come when churches must address core values regarding race relations in the body of Christ as it seeks to finish the task.

THE RACIAL DIVIDE

God, in His wisdom, created the different races of people in His image and likeness. He made each person to reflect His glory in the world. Sin distorts the image of God in people, so people hold to the distortion instead of seeing beauty in the diversity of the races. In the early church, racial division was obvious and had a negative impact, even on some believers. Peter, a Jew, was thrust into an encounter with Cornelius, a Greek, illustrating the racial tension between the Jews and Greeks (Acts 10). God taught Peter an invaluable lesson about race. He learned God values people from every race and shows no partiality (Acts 10:34). He redeems people from every nation, race, and tribe; anyone who fears Him and does what is right is acceptable to Him (Acts 10: 35). Each person who accepts Christ, regardless of race, is recognized as a "child of God."

After Peter's encounter with Cornelius, members of the church in Jerusalem criticized him for crossing the racial line. Peter not only spoke with Gentiles but also ate with them, which was religiously unacceptable (Acts 11:3). Peter learned his Jewishness did not define him and accepted that God was no respecter of persons. God had demolished the race wall that divided Peter and the Gentiles. True to human tendencies, Peter attempted to rebuild the broken down wall that divided the races. At one point, he withdrew himself from the Gentiles because he was afraid of what his fellow Jews would say. This behavior confused the Gentiles, and some Jews were led astray to act hypocritically along with Peter (Galatians 2:11-14). Paul, the apostle, confronted him on this issue and reminded him of the danger this type of division is to the kingdom of God.

People cannot change their race. That is how God created them, everyone in His image after His likeness. When they become followers of Christ, He makes them new in spirit, but they will maintain their racial identity. It is impossible to change that. God, who created them, does not treat them according to race. He judges all people with equity and justifies them by their faith in Christ alone, yet two thousand years later, churches continue to deal with the dysfunction of racial division.

In many spheres of society, it continues to be a challenge for Christians to bridge the racial gap and become one with believers from other races. On their day of worship, churches retreat to their corners with their own kind, gathering in their tribes and making that time, according to some, the most segregated time of the week. This is antithetical to the "Church is one foundation." These church members will testify that people from every race and tribe and language will gather in the presence of God, yet they find it difficult to come together to worship in the here and now. So, in a multi-racial community, each group, Black, Caucasian, Asian, and others, retreats to their corners to worship the same Lord who is not divided.

While all persons bear the image of the sovereign Lord, some people regard themselves as superior to others and twist the Lord's definition of human beings to justify enslaving and discriminating against others they regard as racially inferior. Racism and bigotry breed injustice against others, including fellow followers of Christ. When this is the case, they are devaluing the precious image of the Lord. These self-proclaimed followers of Christ live in the same community, speak the same language, and shop at the same stores. They work together in their secular spaces during the week but find it difficult to worship together in their gathering places on their day of "worship." They allow the enemy to clump them into racial tribes, forgetting their connections in Christ.

The racial divide is broader than styles of worship and cultural preferences. It is a debilitating spiritual and moral problem. Followers of Christ should know the Father gives people who accept Jesus Christ as Lord a new life. They should put off old attitudes and prejudices with the old life and adapt to the new life in Christ. Since God made every person in His image, every follower of Christ should see every person in that light. This often, however, is not the case. There are still people who claim to be members of God's Church who find it difficult to accept and love fellow believers from other races. According to Ed Stetzer, these members have become comfortable with the racial status of their churches.[17] They are happy as they are and not eager to integrate with members of other races. Some go as far as erecting virtual barriers to preserve the status quo and refuse to even talk about obvious racial issues. Christ's image is reflected most clearly among believers when different ethnic groups can worship Him together as one body.

A person's race does not define the person since there is neither Jew nor Greek in Christ (Galatians 3:28). Despite such truth, the Lord identifies the value of each racial group as He informed John in Revelation 7:9, people from every nation, tribe, and language will stand together before His throne. Nonetheless, churches in many areas of society continue to adhere to global systems, finding comfort in congregating under their favored racial banners, with little or no tolerance for those outside their racial definition.

The advancements in social media have made these racial biases become more obvious as churches get caught up in the political frenzies of the day. In 2021, Critical Race Theory (CRT), for example, has become fighting words. CRT is a theory that is used to recognize systemic racial inequity. Yet, some segments of the evangelical community in America use this as a license to fortify their racial position while broadening the divide. These positions, from any perspective, deepen wounds and increase pain while diminishing the value of God's creation. Ignoring the value of human beings created in God's image causes churches to maintain racial divides.

Some people view one race as more valued and often at the expense of others. God created His Church as a force in society to bring people from every race together to worship Him. However, according to David Platt, churches are a force for "continuing [racial division]."[18]

God's Church enhances racial diversity as a way of shining the light of His glory in a segregated society. It accepts Christ's commission to rise above racial division to show His glory to the nations. How are churches doing at bridging the racial gap? Michael Emerson[19] defines a church that is intentional about cultivating racial integration as one where no racial group is over 80% of the congregation. His research suggests that churches continue to be a standard for racial division. While they need to be the unifier of society, Emerson asserts, over 95% of Caucasian Christians gather in "Caucasian churches." Only 5% gather in mixed groups on their day of worship. African American churches are no better. Emerson points out over 90% of people of African descent attend African American churches. He further stated only 8% of all Christian congregations in the United States are racially mixed. How can this be when many of these communities are so racially diverse? Lack of racial connectedness inhibits churches from carrying out the mission among the nations.

Sometimes Christians from one race find it difficult or impossible to even brush shoulders with their neighbors from other races in their community. Yet, they are often eager to go halfway around the world, saying they want to take the Good News to people with whom they do not relate locally. The question is, how can this be Good News for those who are far away and not for those nearby? The time has come for churches to move forward and break down racial walls. This is important if the world will know that followers of Christ are following the real Christ and not just an idea or some ethnic icon. Jesus reminded His followers all people would know they are His followers because they love one another (John 13:35). Our connection to the risen Lord defines the love to which Jesus alluded.

True racial harmony in the local congregation shows it cares about the great multitude from every people and tribe gathering to worship God. It is not enough for Christians in a multi-ethnic community to huddle in churches according to their racial makeup, shining their little light in their little corners. They have the obligation to join with others of different races to gather people from every race whom the Lord is drawing to Himself.

Some local churches move to define themselves by their race and often encourage bigotry and hatred against people from other races who themselves are followers of Christ. Paul taught the Ephesians no one hates his own body (Ephesians 5:29).

Louis, a young law student, was seeking answers to some of life's questions when he walked into a local church in his college town. He recently became a follower of Christ, and attended a local Baptist church. According to him, the message was inspiring and offered answers to some of his questions. At the end of the service, though, he felt invisible since no one noticed him as a first-time visitor. The pastor met him at the door and thanked him for visiting but shocked him by suggesting he look for a church where he could worship with his 'own kind.' This encounter caused him, as a young intellectual, to view the church in a negative light. He saw himself as a child of God, yet he felt the church he visited that day made him feel there must be categories of racial groupings in the kingdom of God. Many local churches testify of their commitment to racial diversity, yet they are far from accommodating people from other races in their assemblies. Or if they do, they relegate these others to subordinate places in the attempt to maintain racial purity. In these instances, churches get together in their different groups as oil and water. With oil and water, the groups come together and engage together but return to their original state. Churches instead should strive to be like sugar and water. As sugar and water, they come together, accept the value of each other and become one together as they move forward to fulfill the mission of the Church. Christ brings everyone who calls on His name into His Church as a living spiritual stone being built up into a spiritual house. He does not consider race or location.

Becoming one body in Christ and being joined to one another makes it possible for people from everywhere to love one another. There are members of churches who despise other Christians because of their race. These members need to remind themselves that Christ connects every believer, regardless of race, tribe, or geographic location, spiritually to one another. There is no room for discrimination and hatred. Believers from every nation, tribe, language, and group become one in Christ.

Existing racial realities impede the progress of the mission, and racial tensions among followers of Christ can do what persecution failed to accomplish. Churches must not rely on secular civil entities to take the lead in initiating frank conversations about the value of persons of different races. It must take the lead in confronting systemic racism and inequity to show the world the righteousness of a holy God. They have the perfect format to bring people together to teach them to understand and empathize with the life experiences of one another.

Many churches are grappling with how to rectify the issue of racial discrimination. In His assessment of the seven churches (Revelation 2-3), the author gave commendation where commendation was necessary. He also highlighted faults but never left them to figure out what to do to correct the faults. He, in most cases, called churches to repent. Churches show true repentance when they sacrifice preferences and obediently respond to God. As they repent, God forgives and restores them to engage in the healing of people's brokenness more broadly.

In the case of racial and ethnic divisions, there will be no resolution until churches view such divisions through spiritual lenses and repent. They must accept God-created diversity of people to partner together to finish the task. With that in mind, churches must review where they stand regarding racial unity. Where they are found wanting, they must repent. They must change their mind, attitude, and behavior. Demeaning people's worth based on race or ethnicity is a sin against the Creator. While not every church is engaged in this sin, it is the responsibility of every church to be aware of the prevalence of this sin and keep calling for repentance. The church at Pergamum (Revelation 2:14) provides a great example. The entire church was not engaged in following Balaam's teaching. Only some among them subscribed to what Balaam was teaching, yet the Lord called the entire church to repent.

The Church must move beyond tolerating one another to accepting and loving one another as valued members of Christ's body.

True repentance will lead churches to become more proactive in bridging the racial gap. Deep, informal, and transparent discussions will lead sisters and brothers beyond tolerance and acceptance to love and harmony. These interactions will help members adjust their thinking about people of other races and guard their conversations as they get to know one another as brothers and sisters in Christ. They will learn to speak kindly about each other regardless of personal and racial experiences, knowing the old has passed and everything has been made new.

As followers of Christ, church members attempt to interact with other believers of different races without being condescending to some, placating those deemed important, or leveling blame for past failures; they are called to reflect Christ. Churches then must break the holy huddle and move from their comfortable spaces to fellowship with sisters and brothers of different races in their spaces. History suggests that the initial attempts to forge better-integrated churches have not been easy. However, it is necessary for members to go beyond the racial and ethnic walls that Christ has already broken down and make it happen. The Holy Spirit Himself will bear witness; they are all children of the same eternal Father (Romans 8:16).

It is necessary to reveal Christ's image to the world, not as Black, White, Asian, or Middle Eastern. The Church must take the lead in showing the world that Christ is love, and this love has no racial identity. When they show the beauty of a loving Father who gave Himself for all people and is reflected in the diversity of races, they are making Him more attractive to the world. Churches must try now and not wait for the glorious appearance of Christ to enjoy the one Church of White, Black, Hispanic, Korean, Chinese, and all other races together.

A DISCIPLE-MAKING MACHINE

"Go therefore and make disciples of all nations, baptizing them in the name of the Father and of the Son and of the Holy Spirit, teaching them to observe all that I have commanded you. And behold, I am with you always, to the end of the age."

—Matthew 28:19-20

Everything the Church does proclaims Jesus as Lord and leads to the creation and multiplication of disciples. Jesus showed how to make disciples and then mandated the extent of the disciple-making effort. He called twelve people to give up their lives, follow Him, and learn to become "fishers of men." Pouring His life in them and teaching them to imitate Him, He used different methodologies and approaches to train them to become disciple-making machines. On the day of Pentecost, the training they received from their Lord paid off. Three thousand persons accepted the message and became part of the Church that day. He had commanded His Church to go everywhere and invite people to follow Him and train those followers to do likewise, beginning in their immediate community and out to every corner of the earth. The task is daunting, but when the Church embraces this mandate and follows the leadership of the Holy Spirit, the Lord will use it to make and multiply disciples.

Many local churches know it is their responsibility to make disciples but sometimes have difficulties fulfilling this mandate. They often think they are doing enough to make people comfortable. They normally rejoice when people accept the gospel and are eager to add new believers to their numbers, but often, that is where the engagement ends.

THINK DISCIPLES, NOT CHURCH MEMBERSHIP

The Church keeps the spiritual harvest in its purview and thinks of disciples rather than church membership. With the commitment to make disciples, it positioned itself in a way that whatever it does leads to multiplying disciples. That is the mandate Christ its owner gave.

There are many churches with good internal programs and excellent teaching materials. Their qualified teachers teach the same group of members for several years, intending to make them "good workers" in the church. Their end goal is to cultivate good church members with a wide array of biblical knowledge who commit themselves to the huddle as regular attendees, sacrificial givers, and supporters of the church's ministries. These are all good things, but something is missing when, after years of learning, members still can not lead a person to the Lord and engage in making disciples. Only those who are growing to maturity will obey Jesus' command to make disciples. Of course, thinking disciples begin with being sure about who Jesus is. When people believe Jesus Christ is Lord, they will listen to and believe what He commands. Many people hear His Word and can speak those words, but do they believe if they are not practicing what they heard? The writer of the letter to the Hebrews affirmed the importance of obeying the Word of the Lord, saying some have had the Good News proclaimed to them, but the message they heard was of no value to them because they did not obey (Hebrews 4:2). Jesus' disciples believe His commands and obey Him.

In making disciples, not only did Jesus give the Good News, but He was also interested in cultivating and maturing His disciples rather than just having a crowd following Him. His goal was always to distinguish between those who were becoming true disciples and those who were following for the thrill. He never sent the crowd to go as lambs among wolves (Matthew 10:16) or to go without money or extra clothes or sandals. He sent only those He was training to become His disciples. With the end in mind, He commanded His disciples to make disciples among people everywhere. No group was exempted. He mobilized and empowered others to make disciples of others as well. He showed this was an ongoing lifestyle process, not just a momentary engagement. His disciples continue to make disciples as they go about their daily lives. As a result, churches should bring people in, teach them a pattern of obedience to the Word of God, and send them out to make disciples. Following this principle helps to train disciples in righteous living as they get the Good News more quickly to the nations.

In thinking disciples, churches need to ask what they want members to become and provide the information, tools, and opportunities required for members to become what they envisioned. They should use every Bible study group, including Sunday school classes and small group time, as tools to cultivate and nurture multiplying disciples. They should use these different situations to create opportunities to enable members to become disciples who will learn to pour their lives into the lives of others. Churches have reasons to rejoice and get excited when a person is drawn to accept Jesus Christ as Lord. After all, there is joy before the angels of God over one sinner who repents (Luke 15:10). They should not stop at welcoming the new spiritual babies. Churches must take responsibility for providing the spiritual nourishment needed to make spiritual babies grow to spiritual maturity. They must teach the new believers how to surrender to the Lord and how to pass what they learned to others.

BECOMING A DISCIPLE-MAKING MACHINE

How can churches become a disciple-making machine? First, they should know the Lord has given them special gifts to equip members to serve one another and to serve in making Him known to people in every nation. They must be intentional about employing best practices to equip and mobilize disciples. Jesus was intentional in the approach He used to make and cultivate those He called to be His disciples. He invited the most unlikely individuals to be part of His small group and poured His life into them as He formed them into disciples. This was difficult with the different personalities, but He stuck with His small group of twelve men, taught them, and cultivated enthusiasm among them. They ended up turning the "world upside down."

Becoming a disciple-making machine begins with prayer, asking the Lord of the harvest to open doors to the gospel and raise workers to go into the harvest. Ralph, a pastor in one South American country, patterned his disciple-making effort after Christ's and showed what it means to be a disciple-making machine. In a short time, he cultivated a large group of disciples by using the multiplication principle. First, he poured his life into nineteen people. Those nineteen were his small group, and they became leaders of their own small group of eight people each. He not only taught and fellowshipped with them, but he also tasked them with the responsibility of training members as they were being trained to start their own groups. In a short time, there was a small group movement happening. To avoid chaos, Pastor Ralph meets one time per week with the leaders of his group for Bible study. All nineteen leaders would take the lesson they learned that week to their group of eight members. Members of these groups must find at least two people to practice what they learned. These can be family members, neighbors, co-workers, or just anyone. Part of the gathering was to share how it was going with their disciple-making effort. As people came to know Christ, the focus was on training them to become disciples while they were making disciples themselves. There was great excitement in the church as every member became a disciple-maker.

Becoming a disciple-making machine means churches must be more interested in why people gather than the number of people showing up for the huddle. Spiritual babies cannot sustain the mission of the Church. The Barna Group agrees with this assessment. According to the survey:

- *One in five persons in America professing to be Christian lives in a way that depends on God.*
- *One out of six people claiming to be followers of Christ is committed to engaging in personal spiritual development.*
- *Most professing Christianity do not know basic teachings and do not act differently because of their alleged conversion.*[20]
- *About 46% of evangelicals—professing Christians—read their Bible only once per week or not at all.*[21]

This dire assessment suggests church members are not being trained to become disciples. Could it be with this attitude, churches are contributing to developing a colony of church members instead of disciples of Christ?

The point of the decision to follow Christ is only the beginning of the journey. This is the beginning of life in God's kingdom and discipleship. The new life in Christ causes repentance and life seeking to become more like Jesus every day. This is what it means to become a disciple of Christ - listening to the Savior's teachings and doing what He commands.

Disciples train themselves in righteousness and keep growing in grace and knowledge of Christ. They learn to place their dependence on the Lord and continue to desire to study to show themselves approved by God. They strive to live their life as the new persons they have become in Christ and are eager to share their new life with others.

The number of those who claim to be Christians should be enough manpower to get the gospel to the remotest corners of the earth. Churches are unable to lead the great multitudes to worship because most church members have not been equipped to become disciples. Churches must equip every member to make disciples who will make disciples and equip these disciples to live out the Great Commandment and fulfill the Great Commission. They can never be satisfied with people coming into the huddle to become spectators. Those coming into the huddle must learn the cost of following Christ. This calls them to give up personal rights and feelings for the sake of obedience to Christ. They must deny self and be personal cross-bearers for the cause of Christ (Luke 9:23).

The Church must be ready to live for Christ, as they are ready to die for Him.

True disciples will follow Christ because they see themselves as dead to the old person and their sin-dominated life and alive to God through Christ. When they consider themselves dead to sin and alive to God, they grow up not allowing sin to rule them.

Sin will always be present, but disciples must not give sin the opportunity to take root and rulership over their lives. Growing disciples want everyone to have a new life in Christ.

EQUIP AND MOBILIZE DISCIPLES

In an age where bigger seems to be better, churches might see the need to form small groups to mold members into disciples. As they empower members to make their own small groups, many more groups will be formed, and the gospel will reach many more people and make them disciples as well. "Small in a big way" leads to each doing their small part to produce big results.

The mandate to make disciples is given to every member who has been entrusted with the word of reconciliation. Since such is the case, churches must teach every member to believe that they are a disciple maker, regardless of their unique spiritual giftedness. No one is exempted. They must prioritize the effort to train and inspire members to get the gospel out as they are going.

Often, people think of making disciples by using "discipleship materials" and classes with fill-in-the-blank texts. These are valuable tools, but when one thinks of making disciples, one does not need to look any further than Jesus and Paul. In equipping His disciples, Jesus emphasized the Father's vision and ensured they were clear about the mission. They saw Him and how He responded in different circumstances as He taught them on the spot and on demand.

With Timothy, Paul not only gave him instructions, but he also gave him important responsibilities. In encouraging the church at Corinth to imitate him, Paul informed them he was sending Timothy to remind them of his way of life in Christ Jesus (1 Corinthians 4:17). Paul believed in Timothy's faith. He trusted Timothy and allowed him to serve with him in the work of the gospel (Philippian 2:22). Timothy followed Paul and learned invaluable lessons that made him a good disciple.

Churches must take the risk and emphasize God's vision and mission instead of focusing on traditional structures. Good old traditions, forms, or structures are no longer expedient. These cannot become the focus of churches that will become disciple-making machines. Churches must be radical in equipping disciples to make disciples of people from where they are to the nations.

Where do churches start in equipping disciples? Eliminating non-essential programs and activities will not be easy, but it will be necessary. Besides developing an education process that includes every member and crosses ministry lines, investing in a Paul-to-Timothy mentoring ministry will be a good idea. This would mean pairing new converts with more seasoned and growing disciples and holding them accountable by giving them opportunities to report progress.

New disciples will learn from what they see and experience. In the mentoring relationships, they will learn to develop habits of holy living, share their faith in Christ, and cultivate concern for those waiting to hear. No one in the church should be excluded from this process because of their role in the assembly. Everyone should know through their service in the assembly that they are being equipped as disciples to make disciples.

Since churches are tasked with making and equipping disciples, members must be clear about the vision. This means all programs and activities must lead to helping members understand why gathering the great multitude to stand before God's throne is their responsibility. Churches must help disciples define their commitment to the mission and continue to communicate ways disciples might fulfill the mission.

Jesus called twelve men to follow Him and equipped them by doing life together in their small groups. They spent quality time together, getting to know one another, practicing building up one another, and learning together. He gave them tools and opportunities to practice what they learned. In the same churches must train members and provide the tools they need to share the Good News first with people they know. They will gather their disciples in other small groups with the goal of expanding the church to the nations.

Members identify and practice their spiritual gifts in these groups as they continue to learn to do the gospel. They recognize that the gospel transcends denominational, racial, cultural, geographical, political, and social boundaries, and it goes beyond just telling people but showing them how much Jesus loves them.

There are many small groups models the local church can adapt to fit its specific situation. It needs to know its community and discern what small group models would work.

Building a network of small groups takes planning and consideration of the overall vision and mission of the church. As core members are trained and equipped, they can take the responsibility of baptizing new converts and immediately start the disciple-making process. In these small groups, they can start holistic ministries to meet physical, emotional, and spiritual needs while training and preparing each person for the mission.

Having equipped the saints for the work of the ministry, churches must be prepared to rally disciples for action. They will encourage disciples to have knowledge of the culture and religious practices of people who are unreached. As part of the mobilization process, different groups in the church can learn more about the people they are praying for. In taking responsibility for these people, church members can examine bridges and barriers that can impede or advance the gospel among the particular focus people. They can continue to educate themselves in their small groups to position themselves to launch appropriate platforms to make it easier for unreached people to hear the Good News. Members are responsible for listening to the Holy Spirit as He leads individuals to serve as church planters and missionaries throughout the nations. It might be to the next city block, village, town, or across the world. The one sure thing is that when churches prioritize gathering the great multitude to stand before God's throne, God will bless and prosper them. Having God's agenda as theirs will bring focus, joy, and vitality to any congregation. He will multiply disciples and expand the Church to the ends of the earth.

EMPOWER DISCIPLES

Jesus equipped, mobilized, and empowered His disciples for the mission without taking them into a formal classroom. He spent three years sharing and preparing them for ministry. He modeled for them, assisted them, and allowed them to practice. Then He left them to do the work after He filled them with the Holy Spirit. His goal was to make them fishers of men. He kept them as real people who could understand and relate to other real people around them and gave them the tools they needed and opportunities to get the job done. He was confident that He had fully equipped them to make, baptize, and educate disciples to obey everything He had commanded.

On the Day of Pentecost, the Holy Spirit baptized Jesus' followers as they waited for Him. He gave them spiritual gifts to build up and sharpen one another for the work of the ministry. He gave apostles, prophets, evangelists, shepherds, and teachers unique gifts to equip members to bring about obedience to propel Christ's name among all nations. Members with these spiritual gifts are only potential apostles, prophets, evangelists, shepherds, and teachers until they begin to practice using their gifts. Churches must allow members to use their spiritual gifts to advance the mission.

While God commanded the Church to train members to become disciples, many local churches delegated this role to seminaries and mission-sending agencies. Nothing is wrong in turning theological and leadership training over to these institutions. Such cooperation represents the interconnectedness of Christ's body which allows sharing of giftedness. The advantage of deferring related training to these institutions is that they provide the best training in their area of giftedness. However, deferring responsibility to these para-church organizations and mission agencies can create degrees of disconnect from the local church. Sometimes this leaves disciples to fend for themselves and defeat the intended purpose. Members' accountability should never be deferred to training institutions and mission agencies.[22] It is the church's responsibility to forge partnerships with these institutions to help identify the giftedness of members while creating opportunities, providing tools, and holding members accountable.

Churches must be intentional about giving every member opportunity to serve. They should identify apostles, prophets, evangelists, pastors, and teachers among members and create the platform from where they might function. As members pray and the Lord intensifies their concern for lost people, the church must lay hands on the ones called out and send them. The church must take responsibility for supporting those who go. The small group might not have resources but can network with others to empower disciples. All are responsible for the harvest. It is a faithful thing to provide financial support to those who are going, even though they might be strangers (3 John 1:5-8). By doing so, members will function in a manner worthy of God. This is true for all areas of giftedness.

Churches must think of different ways to empower disciples to make disciples. One way to do so is to train them to function in the different spheres of society. For example, members of the church who are educators should be encouraged and celebrated as they use their station in life to influence those in their space with the gospel. This practice can be promoted in all the different spheres of society. The church will provide the tools needed for making disciples in these unconventional ways. Churches should also seek to provide the encouragement and support the disciples need.

Functioning in these spheres can be lonely and dangerous. Often, disciples must negotiate dangerous terrains and hostile territories to get the gospel to the waiting souls. Members of the different churches must pray incessantly for one another as they focus on becoming disciple-making machines.

CONCLUSION

For the Lord himself will descend from heaven with a cry of command, with the voice of an archangel, and with the sound of the trumpet of God. And the dead in Christ will rise first. Then we who are alive, who are left, will be caught up together with them in the clouds to meet the Lord in the air, and so we will always be with the Lord. Therefore encourage one another with these words.

—1 Thessalonians 4:16-18

The Church is here to stay until it finishes the mission. The already defeated enemy will continue to wage war against its groups scattered across the globe, but his end is already determined. He has no power against the Church. He has already been consigned to the lake of fire and sulfur, where he will be tormented day and night forever and ever (Revelations 20:10). The Church is already victorious. Victory has already been won! The Church continues to celebrate as it pushes against the gates of hell until every person held captive is released.

Despite the glorious victory, Christ is expecting His Church to stand firm and fight against the distractions of the enemy. He wants His Church to reflect the brightness of His glory among the nations. The enemy wants the Church to relax in its victory and commit spiritual treason. He wants the Church to become complacent because he knows a complacent Church will not take part in God's mission. Complacency in a church compromises the power of the Holy Spirit. No church should delight the enemy by being overly satisfied with itself and its current achievements.

When Eve and Adam rebelled against God, the enemy saw victory, but God expressed His grace to them. He rescued them and preserved humanity, and the war against His kingdom continued. At the great flood, the enemy again saw victory as he orchestrated the destruction of humanity, but God saved eight people; Noah and his family, to continue to preserve humanity for worship. The enemy never stopped! God called Abraham and promised to bless all families on earth through his descendants. His descendants rebelled against God at different junctures, and again, the enemy thought he had won the war. God continued to preserve His creation by His grace because of His purpose for humanity.

Later still, people rejected the God who preserved them and asked for a king to rule them. God gave them their king, who abdicated his responsibility, and God's people were brought under the rule of strange kings who occupied the land God promised them. The people were so wounded they became refugees in their own land and had forgotten God. And the enemy expected victory. God continued to pursue people, wanting to be their God, and the battle continued.

At the proper time, Jesus came as the Lamb of God who took away the sins of the world. Humanity despised and rejected Him. They hid their faces from Him and exclaimed they had no king but Caesar! His very own people condemned Him and sentenced Him to death. They beat Him and humiliated Him, then nailed Him to a cross. The weight of their sin was heaped on Him. The effect of sin was so devastating that He cried, *"My God, my God, why have you forsaken me!"* (Matthew 27:46). He died and was buried, and again the enemy rejoiced! He had won! He claimed victory, not knowing that death and the grave had no power over the Lamb of God, the Savior of humanity. His celebration did not last because Christ, the Redeemer, rose from the dead three days later and sealed the victory. He is alive! He has all authority in earth and heaven, and the fate of the enemy is sealed.

Jesus already did what needed to be done to fulfill God's mission in the world. He defeated the enemy at the cross and sealed the eternal victory. He appointed His Church to join Him in gathering the great multitude from every nation whom He wants to reconcile to Himself. This great multitude will gather to rejoice in the glorious victory and worship the Lord, their Savior. The final victory celebration will come when the trumpet sounds. All who know Christ will be reunited with Him. They shall be changed and put on immortality. The enemy will be banished forever and consigned to eternal damnation, where he will no longer terrorize God's people. The final victory will happen!

The Church comprises broken people, yet God entrusted it with the responsibility to inform all other broken people about the victory that is theirs. It teaches people from every nation despite their continuous rebellion against God. These people do not know they can find forgiveness for their rebelliousness, but the Church never gives up. Seeing everyone informed is a mammoth task, but God has equipped and empowered the Church to complete this mission.

Throughout history, the Church became distracted because of the many missteps. Sometimes it has been dragged through the abyss of scandals where eradication or societal uselessness seemed eminent. Thieves who have come to steal, kill, and destroy have tried to hijack the Church but failed. The enemy continues his effort to entice it with the shiny trinkets of secularism and materialism, but its owner is watching. He will not allow His Church to fall into Satan's icy grips. He will keep it holding fast to the foundation upon which it has been built and be serious about the mission of its owner.

Sensing defeat, the enemy launched the deadly weapons of division and complacency in the Church. He wants to see a compromising Church. God, however, has intercepted these attacks through His Holy Spirit. He keeps His Church safe and secure to complete the mission. His people will rise and shine the light of His glory across the nations, and nothing will stop them. Considering this eternal victory, the Church remains vigilant and continues to storm the gates of hell. Members have relinquished the lead to the Holy Spirit, who is gathering the great multitude Christ purchased with His own blood.

Christ is "polishing" His Church to reflect His image brightly beyond the boundaries of orthodoxy to the billions of people who are still waiting to make Jesus Christ Lord. It is always evaluating its structures and identifying those that prove to be counterproductive to the mission. It relinquishes debilitating structures that enhance security and comfort since these are the "go-to" corners and are barriers to its expansion.

The Church recognizes counterproductive practices for what they are and abolishes them. This often is painful but must be done for the sake of God's mission. Abolishing unnecessary structures helps to propel the Church from where it is, to where it needs to be.

A disciple-making Church celebrates Christ's victory. It sees the harvest, and nothing stands in its way. It shows its delight in the Lord by spreading the Good News to reap the harvest. Keeping the mission in mind, it forms networks and collaborates to train disciples who also train disciples all over the world. It uses its local branches to strategically equip, mobilize, and empower disciples everywhere to do the same.

The entire community of faith is being shaken in different ways, and in the end, only the true Church will stand as it ends the time out and breaks the huddle to finish the task.

Go Church! Go! Keep breaking the huddle and go. As you are going, go to nations across the street and around the world. Go to your neighbors and to strangers! Make known the one true God and Jesus whom He sent. Proclaim this great Gospel of the kingdom throughout the entire world as a testimony to all nations so that the end will come. Go, and gather the great multitude of worshippers to stand in victory before His throne!

END NOTES

1. "Church" in the document is used in reference to the universal undefiled body of Christ.

2. Turnover: when a team loses possession of the ball resulting from a steal, going out of bounds, committing a violation, or committing an offensive foul and the opposing team takes possession of the ball.

3. In the early church period, people used the word ìchurch" to include secular gatherings. Christians in the New Testament used the word to mean the assembling of God's called out people. Gene Getz pointed to the difficulty of differentiating between the uses of the word ecclesia. According to him, the word ìchurch" occurred 115 times in the New Testament. Getz suggested the word referred three times to assemblies of people who were not followers of Christ (Acts 19:32,39,41) and twice to the children of Israel (Acts 7:38, Hebrews 2:12). The remaining 110 times the word defines loyal followers of Christ. ìChurch as used in this document defines the universal body, in that true followers around the world are brought into a community to singularly reflect the image of Christ. While God's Church will always prevail against the onslaught of the enemy, local church groups often fall victims of his attacks.

4. Every person alive is a potential citizen of heaven. John 3:16 points to the fact that God loves the entire world that He gave His one and only Son to die so who believes in Him should have everlasting life.

5. Joshuaproject.net; Joshua Project is a research initiative seeking to highlight people groups of the world with the fewest followers of Christ. Accurate, updated people group information is critical for understanding the progress the Church is making and for completing the Great Commission. A great multitude from every tribe, tongue, nation, and people will stand before the Throne in worship to God (Revelation 7:9)

6. There was only one Bible in this group. This was not even a complete Bible but was only portions that were smuggled into the country. They demonstrated what is meant by hiding God's Words in their heart by memorizing the portions they had.

7. Finishing the Task (FTT finishthetask.com) is an association of mission agencies and churches who want to see reproducing churches planted among every people group in the world. According to them, in 2006, they identified over six hundred unreached, unengaged people (UUP) groups with populations above 100,000. Twelve years later in 2018, it has been reported that a number of these original people groups have been engaged. Many local churches around the world are doing a great job in introducing Christ to groups of people who have no other way of knowing. There is a good possibility the task would have already been finished if every local church were involved.

8. Deuteronomy 4:29 - Local assemblies often mistake the curiosity of people in the harvest as disinterest. However, their curiosity is their way of searching for answer to their life questions. The Lord made it clear that people who seek Him will find Him, if they searched after him with all their heart and with all their soul.

9. Johann Christof Arnold, ìRestoring the Image of God.î
    http://www.plough.en/topics/life/marriage/restoring-the-
    image-of-god

10. 1993 American biographical musical drama film directed
    by Brian Gibson, from a screenplay written by Kate Lanier,
    based on the life of American singer Tina Turner.

11. KASASA Online publication, April 2019. Gen X: Gen X was
    born between 1965 - 1979 and is between 40-54 years old
    (82 million people in U.S.) Gen Y: Gen Y, or Millennials,
    were born between 1980 and 1994. They are between 25-39
    years old. Gen Y.1 = 25-29 years old (31 million people in
    U.S.) Gen Y.2 = 29-39 (42 million people in U.S.) Gen Z:
    Gen Z is the newest generation to be named and was born
    between 1995 and 2015. They are between 4-24 years old
    (nearly 74 million in U.S.)

12. The backdoor syndrome is used to describing the number
    of people being added to the gathering but leave not long
    afterwards. Many churches are doing a good job getting
    people in the front door, but for many reasons, they dis-
    continued attending.

13. This young man understood Christianity in the context of
    religious and secular and the two do not mix. Outside the
    religious circle he had to interact with the secular on the
    job, among his peers and out in the community in general.
    His understanding created spiritual competition and those
    competing ideologies caused him to give up the religious.

14. An alarming number of former churchgoers are falling away
    to become members of other religious groups. Many young
    men across the Caribbean are falling away from the Church
    to follow the teachings of Rastafarianism. Many at the same
    time are being attracted to atheism preferring to relinquish
    their Christian upbringing for the ideology of ìno God.î

15. The pastor did not make it clear how he would ìkill the way-ward sheep." The statement gave the impression he was the owner of the ìflock."

16. 2 Peter 1-3, But false prophets also arose among the people, just as there will be false teachers among you, who will se-cretly bring in destructive heresies, even denying the Master who bought them, bringing upon themselves swift destruc-tion. And many will follow their sensuality, and because of them the way of truth will be blasphemed. And in their greed, they will exploit you with false words. Their condem-nation from long ago is not idle, and their destruction is not asleep.

17. Edward John Stetzer is an American author, speaker, re-searcher, pastor, church planter, and Christian missiologist.

18. https://churchleaders.com/news/323741-david-platt-asks-why-is-t4g-so-white.html

19. The Multiracial Congregations Project http://hirr.hartsem. edu/org/faith_congregations_research_multiracl.html

20. Barna, George, ìTop trends of 2011.

21. Ibid

22. Mission entities such as Youth With A Mission (YWAM) and International Mission Board (IMB) are made up of peo-ple from churches but operate separate from these churches.